Teachers Are Made, Not Born

Growing Successful Teachers In Your Church

STANDARD PUBLISHING®
Cincinnati, Ohio 18-03174

Dedicated . . .

To all the staff and scores of Sunday-school teachers and workers of Central Christian Church, St. Petersburg, Florida, who have gone the second mile during the last twenty years.

To our family who has given us unconditional support.

Editorial assistance for this volume was provided by:
Robert D. Massie,
President/Founder,
Dynamics of the Biblical World, Inc.

Library of Congress Cataloging-in-Publication Data

Fine, Eddie, 1938—
Fine, Billye Joyce, 1941—
Teachers Are Made, Not Born: Growing Successful Teachers In Your Church/
by Eddie and Billye Joyce Fine

ISBN 0-87403-624-0: $9.95
1. Christian education—teacher training

BV1533.F53 1990 90-31369
268'.3—dc20 CIP

Contents

Foreword

Teachers Are Made, Not Born is a book that is needed by everyone involved in Christian education. It is the book we have been waiting to have in our hands for many years!

During the last forty years I have been involved in Christian education in churches with attendance ranging from one hundred to five thousand. This book will be a valuable tool in churches of all sizes. It will meet the needs of new and inexperienced teachers and at the same time will challenge the experienced teacher.

Teachers Are Made, Not Born should be required reading in college classes related to Christian education. It will assist administrators in the process of recruitment and training. It is applicable to all age levels. It is written in clear, concise style. It deals with issues that are regularly encountered in all churches. Volunteers, as well as professional educators will benefit from the time invested in reading this book.

Get ready for an experience that will enhance your Christian education ministry. As you read, you will be motivated and encouraged. You will receive specific help that will enable you to share God's Word in a way that will change the lives of your learners.

Barbara Bolton

1

"To teach is to learn."
—Japanese Proverb

Teachers Are Made, Not Born

"Joe! Joe!"

Betty raised her voice above the din of a hundred "how are yous" and at least that many "have a good afternoons." The hall of the church following the worship service wasn't the best place to carry on a conversation, but she wanted to ask how Joe's new teaching job was going.

She finally got his attention. "How are those fifth-grade boys?" she asked, as she wiggled past two ladies that had planted themselves in the center of the corridor.

Are You a Good Teacher?

"They're great, Betty. I really enjoy them, but I'm not sure about how good I am at teaching." Joe seemed very glad that she cared enough to ask.

Joe, a thirty-five-year-old engineer, had been teaching a class of fifth-grade boys in the Junior Department for about three months. Betty's been a teacher for almost twenty-five years and is known around the church as one of the best. Over the years, many of the children and adults, Joe included, have drawn closer to the Lord because of Betty's commitment to teaching.

Do You Ever Feel Frustrated? Inadequate?

"Betty, I'm just frustrated every week. I spend time preparing my lesson, I pray for the boys, I try to be sensitive to them, but I always feel like I go in to the class without the slightest idea of what I'm supposed to be doing.

"The boys are fine. I mean they are boys. They do act up sometimes, and sometimes it's obvious that they are bored. But they're great.

"I just feel inadequate. I'm an engineer. Give me the go-ahead and enough time, and I'll see that the finest bridge in the world is built. But give me a class of boys and the privilege of teaching them the most important thing in the world and I just can't cut the mustard. Or at least I don't feel like I can."

Joe's response was a bit of a surprise. "Well, Joe, what's the problem?" Betty was concerned.

"I'm not sure. I try to be the kind of teacher I remember you and others being, but I don't think I'm succeeding. It's like I'm missing something, and I don't even know what it is. In fact, I'm trying to decide whether to continue after the next quarter or to quit and do something I'm more comfortable doing. Any advice?"

Betty listened intently as Joe told his story. Inside a smile was forming because she identified with him. She knew that feeling of inadequacy well. She had struggled with it herself.

Warning Signs

But right alongside the inner smile was a little warning light blinking on and off. She wanted to respond to Joe with the right advice, realizing that his frustration certainly would influence his success as a teacher. It's hard to keep giving your best when you feel inadequate.

But Betty was concerned for another reason. This kind of attitude was a warning that if Joe couldn't resolve the problem, he probably would drop out of teaching and be hesitant ever to try it again. Or worse, it might even affect his willingness to serve the Lord in other ways. Betty knew lots of "Joes" whose willing service had turned into pew-sitting apathy simply because they had had a frustrating experience like this one.

Betty stepped back, rubbed her chin thoughtfully, and said, "Joe, I understand how you feel. I've been there myself. I have a few thoughts popping into my mind that I'm tempted to share with you, but this is too important for a quick conversation.

"I want to pray about it and discuss it with a friend whom I respect. Give me a couple of days, and I'll get back to you."

Do you know Joe? Most teachers in most churches are like

Joe—capable, intelligent, committed people who never really feel good about their contribution to the teaching of God's Word.

You may even be like Joe.

Do you know Betty? Thankfully there are quite a few Bettys around too. You may even be like Betty.

How Were You Taught?

Joe and Betty are examples of the two kinds of teachers in every church. Now, that's not the same as "good" and "bad." It's not that easy. Not even "effective" or "ineffective" best describes the two categories. There's no doubt that God uses Joe with his class. After all, He has used more unlikely vessels than Joe for His purposes.

No, the best way to describe the two is with two phrases. The first category is typified in the phrase: YOU TEACH THE WAY YOU WERE TAUGHT.

That's not too surprising, is it? It's true about virtually everything in life. You speak the way you were spoken to. If you were raised in the northeastern part of the United States, your speech sounds different than that of someone raised in the deep south.

You eat the way your family ate. (Is your childhood favorite Jambalaya or fresh salmon?) You drive the way you were driven. (When was the last time you drove toward town on the left side of the road?) And the list could go on.

Lecture or Discussion?

In that list would be the fact that you teach the way you were taught. If you have learned primarily through a lecture approach, then as a teacher it is very difficult for you even to conceive of a classroom setting where your verbal instruction is not the dominant element. Yes, there may be questions raised by the class and a few well-spoken comments added by class members, but they all revolve around your presentation. That is true whether you are teaching children who are four years old or middle adults.

On the other hand, if you cut your teeth in the discussion/learner involvement environment of the past twenty years, then your concept of the classroom is very different. You probably see the role of the teacher as one who draws people out, helping them to express themselves in a variety of ways. Tell the Bible story to third graders, then get them talking about what they think about it. Or, express a controversial view of an issue or a Bible passage to teens or adults and watch them become involved in meaningful discussion.

You teach the way you were taught. That is a normal and natural thing, but that's not all there is to being an effective teacher, and you realize it. So does Joe. That phrase describes him to a "T." That's why he is typical of most church teachers—capable, intelligent, committed people who are doing their best at a task for which they have had little training. They are teaching the way they were taught.

Which Describes You?

Is that you, too? Let's make some assumptions about you and your motives as a teacher and see if it is. You read them to see if they describe you:

• You love Jesus; you deeply appreciate His great sacrifice and the gift of eternal life; and you are committed to serving Him as He leads you. You are willing to do something in ministry for others, not just attend worship services as a spiritual consumer.

• You have felt His leading in the area of Sunday school or other Bible teaching. You want to do the very best possible job for the Lord, for your learners, and for yourself. Deep down, giving anything but your best is troubling.

• You don't have specialized training in education (that is, you never attended college classes for teachers). You are not a professional teacher, and in your class, you teach the way you were taught.

• You are giving several hours a week in preparation, class time, and planning to your teaching ministry. Or if you are a prospective teacher, you are prayerfully considering the commitment of these hours from your busy schedule.

• You feel a need to be a better teacher than you now perceive yourself to be. You want to be more effective, but because you have no special training, you're not sure how to be.

Volunteers Are Indispensable

Does that sound like you? Congratulations! You are a typical volunteer teacher. Our hats are off to you and the hundreds of thousands like you who make Sunday school the most important Bible teaching "place" in the world. In fact, if it weren't for you and all the others like you, the work of God would be set back seriously. There simply is no other organization or movement in the world that reaches more people on a more consistent basis for more of their lifetimes than the Sunday school.

Then there is the second category of teacher, represented by Betty. No, it's not the I've-been-around-and-have-it-all-together type. It's the kind of teacher described in this phrase: TEACHERS ARE MADE, NOT BORN.

This is the kind of teacher who begins his teaching service like Joe. Those five assumptions you just read are also true of these people. The difference is that they do not operate only on their natural ability. They begin by teaching the way they were taught, but they continue by growing and developing the gift God gave them.

That's easy to say, but the real question is, "How do you do that?" You, as the reader of this book, obviously want to be in that category or you never would have started reading it. Moving you from category one to category two, or confirming you as a solid category two, is our goal.

The first step in the process is for you to realize that every other teacher, including the one at the top of your admiration list, has struggled with the same ambivalence—wanting to be the kind of teacher God wants you to be but at the same time feeling inadequate, unskilled, and somehow not up to the task. The simple fact is that teachers are made, not born.

Beginning right where you are, prospective or current teacher, you can overcome the misgivings and become a good teacher, one whom God will use in the ministry of changing lives through the study of His Word!

The next step is to get a handle on the basics. These are simple principles that you will use immediately to improve your teaching; they are the same simple ideas that will be the basis of a lifetime of growth and development.

Six Principles

We have laid out these simple principles in six, easy-to-remember categories and have given them some familiar names:

WHO?	(You, the learner, and your fellow teachers)
WHAT?	(Our subject matter and the tools we use)
WHEN?	(Wisely using the time we have)
WHERE?	(The learning environment)
WHY?	(The reason we do what we do)
HOW?	(Using methods effectively)

OK! So, teachers are made, not born. Let's get started making you a better teacher. To do that we need to go back to Joe and Betty.

Like so many families whose mom or dad gets involved in a Sunday morning ministry, Betty's family always rode home after church without her. She never was ready to leave when they were—too much to do. As she made her way to the car, she prayed for Joe and decided to stop by that respected friend's house on her way home.

You are Betty's friend. Imagine that she drops by your house and tells you about her conversation with Joe. She believes that Joe has four options:

What Option Do You Choose?

1) If Joe has been at the task for three months and hasn't really felt that he's accomplished anything, maybe the Lord is letting him know that teaching is not his gift. Joe should resign before he loses heart, then find another area of service in which to be involved.

2) Joe has been on the job for three months. He's still feeling his way around. He committed himself for a year. He should stick with it at least that long to see if he can become a more effective teacher.

3) Joe has some natural ability, but the only introduction to teaching he has ever had was what he got as a student. He should stick with it for the year, but get some good input to help him build on whatever natural ability he has.

4) Joe needs to feel that he is contributing to the work of the Lord and not that he is detracting from it. He obviously is very concerned about people studying the Bible but will probably drop out if things don't change. Joe should be encouraged to bow out of the teaching role and step into a support role, like Sunday-school superintendent.

After explaining each of these options, Betty looks at you and says, "Which one of these would you recommend?"

If You Choose Number One

That certainly is conventional wisdom, and you would have a lot of company. But it wouldn't do Joe any good, and it certainly wouldn't be the best situation for the boys. Joe is a very capable person who obviously has a heart for his learners and for the Bible. He's too valuable for any teaching staff to lose. Remember, TEACHERS ARE MADE, NOT BORN!

Go back and select another response, one that will help Joe succeed in being faithful to God's calling.

If You Choose Number Two

You are right when you say that Joe hasn't been at it long enough to see the results he's hoping for. And he has made a commitment. Hanging in there and doing his best is far better than giving up and heading back to the pew.

But you missed one key idea: Joe has the heart for the job, but he has not been adequately prepared to succeed. He's a successful engineer because he has natural ability plus good training. Continuing to teach might keep him from feeling guilty about being a quitter, but unless he has some help and guidance, he won't be any better in twelve months than he is in three months. He won't have fifty-two weeks' experience as a teacher. He'll have one week's experience fifty-two times.

Remember, TEACHERS ARE MADE, NOT BORN! Go back and choose another option that will build Joe up in his new calling and make him more successful.

If You Choose Number Three

Right you are! You are a wise counselor. You realize the truth in Solomon's words: "Instruct a wise man and he will be wiser still; teach a righteous man and he will add to his learning" (Proverbs 9:9).

Joe has what it takes to be a good volunteer teacher. He just needs help and guidance to develop the gift God gave him.

There are many ways to get that help. Books such as this are great places to start. A regular teacher training/planning meeting at his church would be invaluable. Add to that special training events like area-wide seminars, observation of other successful teachers, filmstrips, videos, and the like, and you have the kind of input that over time will make Joe the best teacher he can be. Joe will get the help he needs; the church will keep a good teacher on its staff; and those fifth-grade boys will enjoy a year of life-changing Bible study.

Now that you have given Betty the best possible advice, look below and we'll wrap up this chapter.

If You Choose Number Four

Not a bad observation. It might well be that Joe would be a better administrator than a teacher. But it also may be that Joe's gift of administration is as poorly developed as his gift of teaching. Besides, if he moves into an administrative role in the Sunday school after having difficulty as a teacher, he might empathize with his staff of teachers, but he will never be able to help them with the same frustrations. Remember, TEACHERS ARE MADE, NOT BORN!

No, Joe needs to bloom where he's planted. Go back and choose another option that will help him do that.

If you are like most readers, you thought, "Well, it's obvious that #3 is the right answer. Who would give Joe the kind of advice in those other answers."

The Best Advice

The sad but true fact is that while #3 is the best advice, it is the one piece of advice that is given to the "Joes" of this world the least. We have sat through innumerable Sunday-school staff and Board of Christian Education meetings where numbers 1, 2, and 4 were the only options raised as the groups discussed one of their "Joes."

That's precisely why in most churches many teachers are like Joe and not like Betty.

But the wisdom in #3 was easy for you to see for reasons other than "It's obvious." You had a chance to think about the idea of teachers feeling inadequate. You met one whom you probably liked and related to, and you had a chance to hear what we have to say about it. That helped you make the best choice.

Have you learned anything about teaching yet? We hope so! We hope you clearly see there are two kinds of teachers: those who teach the way they were taught, depending entirely on natural ability; and those who are made, not born, growing and developing the gift God gave.

We hope you also realize why you chose the best advice for Joe. It is not because it is naturally the most obvious or because it is the most commonly given. Neither of those assumptions is true.

The reason you chose the best advice is because we guided you through all the options. We wanted you to be successful, so we helped you make the right choice.

That is exactly what you want to do in your classroom, only in relation to the Bible and not to principles of teaching. You want to be an authoritative guide to help people, young or old, to think about the truth of God's Word for themselves so that when faced with options in life, they too will make the right choices and live lives pleasing to the Lord Jesus.

So again, congratulations! You have picked up two of the most important ideas about teaching that you will ever encounter. They will serve as part of your foundation as we work together to see that you become a teacher who is MADE, NOT BORN.

2

"Without a vision,
The people perish."
— Proverbs 29:18

Teacher, Know Thyself

After a delicious New-York-style cheesecake, and a good forty-five minutes of catching up with each others' personal lives, Betty got down to business.

"Joe, in the hall on Sunday I promised that I would think about the problem you're facing in your teaching and seek some good advice. I've prayed for you and spoken to my husband and a good friend about the problem. We are agreed on the options you have as well as on the option we would recommend to you."

Love Is Fundamental

"Thank the Lord!" exclaimed Sally, Joe's wife. "I've had to live with his worrying for weeks now. He loves those boys and genuinely enjoys being with them, but he just hasn't gotten a handle on teaching them the Bible."

"I've been thinking since Sunday, too." Joe said. He obviously was in a better frame of mind. "I want to teach. I believe the Lord wants me to teach. I believe that it is very important for children, youth, and adults to be studying God's Word. But I don't want to do a poor job of it. I need some help."

Betty was delighted. "Joe, you don't realize it, but that is exactly the advice I was going to give you. I shared our hallway conversation with my husband and with a friend whose advice I respect. We agree that you have what it takes, but like everyone else, you need to learn more about teaching to develop your God-given gift."

"I agree! Well, I mean I agree that I do need to learn more. That sounded like I was tooting my own horn, didn't it?" Chuckles were heard from around the room. "Anyway, I agree. But where do I start?"

Betty piped up, "Do you remember a famous quotation; I think it's from Shakespeare? It goes, 'Know Thyself!' Joe, that's the starting point.

Take a Personal Inventory

"When you come to realize TEACHERS ARE MADE, NOT BORN and you are ready to be 'made,' then it's a good thing to take a little personal inventory to make sure you know exactly where you're starting."

"Then I should have a good start on the process because I think about what I *haven't* got every time I prepare a lesson."

"No, Joe. You miss my point. I don't mean you should keep focusing on the shortcomings that are a problem to you. I mean you should identify what you *do* have, in terms of your commitment and your teaching style." Betty was determined to help.

"I don't think I understand exactly what you mean."

Dave, Betty's husband, had been sitting quietly, enjoying the conversation and the feeling of comfortable fullness from the cheesecake. He, too, had been a teacher for a long time. He liked Joe and wanted to see him do well. Dave leaned forward and spoke.

Why Are You Teaching?

"What Betty means is that you should know why you are teaching, *and* you should know why you do things the way you're doing them now. You can't make too much headway in the right direction until you know where you are. You can't get from 'here' to 'there' if you don't know where 'here' is."

"Thanks, Dave. That's exactly what I mean." Betty liked her husband's gift for getting to the point.

Commitment Commitment Commitment!

Dave continued, "Have you heard the old joke about football being the game where 60,000 people, desperately in need of exercise, sit and watch twenty-two men, desperately in need of rest? The difference between the twenty-two and the 60,000 is COMMITMENT. Those few men are willing to pay the price to do their best in a game, a mere game, while the 60,000 are only willing to pay enough to sit and watch.

"But like football, or basketball, or music, or art, or any other field of human endeavor, people generally don't begin with the kind of commitment those twenty-two have. Why? Because people just starting out rarely have the same vision for something that long-timers have.

"Let me give you an example. Joe, why did you want to teach this year?"

Joe leaned back and thought for a minute. "Well, to be honest, I didn't really want to. I mean, I didn't go and volunteer. George Roush stopped me in the hall one day, told me that they needed a teacher for boys in the Junior Department, and asked me if I would do it. I believe in Bible study, and I've always liked children, so after praying about it for a week or so, I said 'yes.'"

"O.K." Dave said. "Betty, why did you want to teach this year? After all, this is not your first time."

Without hesitating Betty said, "Because I've seen God work in the lives of people in big and little ways over the years. He has actually used me, little insignificant me, to bring people to Him and to help them grow in Him. I can't imagine not teaching."

"And there, Joe, is the difference. Almost everyone begins right where you are. They know there's a need, and they are willing to give of themselves to fill it. As they carry out that responsibility, one of two things happens: their commitment either leads them to seek out help to grow, to develop skills, and to watch with ever-sharper eyes for what God is doing in their learners' hearts, or their commitment leads them to do their duty.

Teaching Is a Joy!

"For one, teaching becomes a joy. Yes, it's a joy that has a price tag of time and energy, but it's still a joy. Over time there is a growing commitment to the 'vision' and a growing willingness to be involved. For the other, there may be enjoyment along with frustration, but the larger vision is never gained. Sooner or later, steam runs out, and the 'duty' is abandoned."

Joe was quiet for a minute, then he spoke up. "That's a very good point. I could see enough of the 'vision' to get me involved in the 'duty,' but the 'duty' has been getting the best of me because I'm not too well equipped. When you put it that way, it makes me want to know more about teaching."

Know Thyself

What about you, reader?

Take a minute to "Know Thyself" a bit better. On the following page are three scales ranging from 1–10. Mark an "X" on each scale in the place that best describes the motivation for your commitment to teaching.

WHEN I WAS FIRST RECRUITED AS A TEACHER, I RESPONDED BECAUSE OF:

DUTY									VISION
1	2	3	4	5	6	7	8	9	10

AT THE END OF MY FIRST YEAR OF TEACHING, THE THING I SENSED THE MOST WAS:

DUTY									VISION
1	2	3	4	5	6	7	8	9	10

RIGHT NOW MY VISION FOR WHAT GOD IS DOING IN MY CLASS AND IN THE SUNDAY SCHOOL IN GENERAL IS:

DUTY									VISION
1	2	3	4	5	6	7	8	9	10

How Is Your Vision?

Take a minute to look at the three scales. What do they tell you about yourself as a teacher? What can you learn about your own motivations? Are you more like Joe or Betty? Have you been able to see what God is doing in your class above and beyond the routine?

If after placing the "Xs" on the page, this book is tilting to the left, weighed down by heavy duties, take heart. That's where most people begin. Even in the Bible, most of the characters were hesitant heroes who responded first out of a sense of duty.

Thank God for whatever it was inside that motivated you to become a willing volunteer in the tremendously important work of the Sunday school. Build on that commitment, develop your skills, watch for God's hand, and enjoy the excitement that a vision of God at work engenders.

This is a very simple exercise. The importance of this kind of evaluation cannot be overstated. The Scripture says, "Where there is no vision, the people perish" (Proverbs 29:18a). We have seen good, committed teachers perish in their teaching and drop out because duty grew larger than vision. On the other hand, people who were not extraordinarily gifted, yet whose vision of God at work grew, have become some of the finest teachers we know.

An Example

In 1972, for example, a young mother registered her children for one of the first Vacation Bible Schools we directed at Central Christian, just two years after we first arrived. She knew nothing about teaching. She just felt that if her children were going to benefit from the VBS, she wanted to be involved. She and her children had a happy, meaningful experience.

Sometime after that first exposure, we asked her to teach Sunday school. She hesitated. Participating in a week of VBS was a whole lot different from regularly teaching in Sunday school. But, remembering the VBS experience and how much her children had learned about God, she said "yes."

We didn't hand her a quarterly, pat her on the back, and say, "Good Luck!" We put her into a class with several experienced teachers who were striving to be the best they could be. She saw good teaching. She participated in training sessions to learn about good teaching. She planned with her department to implement good teaching. Her skill grew, and so did her vision for the importance of the Sunday school.

Now, in 1990 as we write this book, eighteen years after that willing, but inexperienced young mother volunteered for VBS, she is the director of the five-year-old department of the Sunday school at Central Christian.

On top of that, she grew so much that we hired her as an assistant in Central's Christian Day School. After fifteen years, she is now an administrative assistant. Her vision and her personal growth have been exceptional.

"More coffee?" Betty loves entertaining.

Joe and Sally both declined, but Dave extended his cup with a grateful smile. He loves being entertained. It motivates him to conversation. "Joe, I think you've got a handle on this issue of vision and personal motivation. You really should spend time every month or so just getting in touch with where your heart is. It will help a lot. But when you are thinking about 'Knowing Thyself' as a teacher, you can't stop there."

"I hope not," Joe responded.

Why Do You Teach the Way You Do?

"No, you have to go on. Once you've figured out why you're doing what you're doing, you need to think about why you do it the way you do. Why is it that you prefer showing pictures with the Bible story when someone else likes to get up and dramatize it as they go. You know what I mean?"

"Isn't that because we teach the way we were taught?" Joe was proud that he had remembered.

"Exactly!" Betty interrupted. "Over the years you have been

exposed to thousands of different learning experiences, some good, some bad, some neutral. During that time you developed what experts call a 'learning style' or a 'learning preference.' You were born with certain tendencies, but the learning experiences you have had shape and define them.

What Is Your Learning Style?

"There are a lot of different ways that professional educators describe these preferences, but the easiest way to remember them is with three simple words:

- HEARING
- SEEING
- DOING

"Some people prefer learning experiences in which HEARING information or interpretation is primary. Others like SEEING information on a chalkboard, in story pictures, a filmstrip, a video, and the like. Others still like to learn by DOING drama, making diagrams, drawing pictures, imagining themselves in the situation.

"Most everyone prefers one of these over the other two. Most teachers unwittingly bring the same bias to their classrooms. They teach their learners using the style they prefer much more than the other two. But the problem is that not all their learners share their preference, so everyone ends up being more or less frustrated."

Sally spoke up, "You mean like serving three courses of that delicious cheesecake at a sit-down meal?"

"That's right." Betty was glad she was getting through.

"Now I'm not much with the technical side of these matters. I'll leave that to Betty," said Dave. "But I can give you a real simple illustration. Remember that football team and the twenty-two men in need of rest? Imagine that when they were in training, the coach only told them what the plays were. He picked up ideas by hearing them and figured everybody else should too. What kind of a team would he have if his players had just had the plays described to them?"

Since Joe had played football in high school and college, he responded. "The team would never get off the practice field. Some plays are far too complicated to pick up just by hearing them."

"Then what does a *good* coach do?" Dave continued.

"Well, my college coach would explain a play, write it out in a play book, draw it on a chalkboard, show us a film of some other team doing it, and sooner or later actually line us up on a field and guide us through it." A smile began to appear on his face.

Sally chimed in, "Sounds like a wise teacher to me. You heard it, saw it, and did it."

"That really makes sense," Joe said. "I could never get it when he explained the plays to us. I just couldn't see it in my mind. But when he picked up the chalk and drew it on the board, I had it. Even now I love it when during ballgames the TV commentators draw lines on the screen to help you get more out of the instant replay."

"I think you've got the idea, Joe." Betty was on a roll now. "When I said that you should 'Know Thyself' as a teacher, I meant you should be in touch with your motivations *and* your basic teaching style. When you have a handle on those two things, you can do a better job of assimilating what you learn about teaching into your actual practice of teaching."

Do You Teach For All Styles?

"I really see what you mean, Betty. Dave's example brought it to life for me. But now I have a question. In football, I learned best by seeing. So does that mean seeing is my learning preference and the style I lean toward in teaching?"

"Good question! It might mean that, but there's an easy way to take stock of yourself so that you can know for sure." With that, Betty got up, crossed the room, and picked up some papers she had neatly stacked on top of the piano. "This is a learning styles checklist that will help you put your finger on your preference."

"Oh, no. A test!" Joe moaned.

Sally laughed, "Well, it's a cinch that 'doing' is not one of his choices."

"Sally, I think you already have a good idea of what this is all about." Betty was thoroughly enjoying herself. She was so pleased that the Christopher's had taken time to come by this evening. She was equally glad she had stopped Joe in the hall on Sunday.

Discover Your Preference

Now reader, it's your turn. While Joe and Sally take time to discover their learning preferences, you take a few minutes to do the same.

Printed below is the same checklist that the Christopher's are completing. The purpose is to help you determine whether you learn best by seeing, hearing, or doing, or by a combination of those methods.

Please read the three statements in each category below, then check the *one* statement in each category which most closely describes your preference. Don't worry about right or wrong answers. Just check the one that seems most like you.

Personal Checklist of Learning Style Preferences

Learning Style

____ 1. I learn best by watching a demonstration.

____ 2. I learn best by listening to instructions from others or saying the instructions to myself.

____ 3. I learn best by doing things.

Reading

____ 1. I like description; sometimes I stop reading and stare into space, imagining the scene in the book.

____ 2. I enjoy what characters say; I generally skip over lengthy descriptions and illustrations. I like plays and tend to move my lips when I read.

____ 3. I don't especially enjoy reading. I prefer stories where action occurs early. I find move around when I read.

Spelling

____ 1. I recognize words by sight.

____ 2. I sound out words.

____ 3. I write a word to see if it "feels" right.

Handwriting

____ 1. I generally have good handwriting; its appearance is important to me.

____ 2. I write lightly and/or say the words as I write them.

____ 3. I push hard on the pen or pencil when I write; I can write neatly if I try.

Memory

____ 1. I remember faces but forget names; I must write things down to remember them.

____ 2. I remember names but forget faces. I can remember things just by saying them over to myself.

____ 3. I remember best what I do.

Distractibility

____ 1. I am generally aware of sounds around me.

____ 2. I am distracted by movement or visual disorder.

____ 3. I am generally unaware of sounds or movements.

Problem Solving

____ 1. I plan in advance; I organize my thoughts by writing them down; I list problems; I am deliberate.

____ 2. I talk problems out; I try solutions orally. I can talk myself through a problem.

____ 3. I attack a problem physically; my solutions are usually those involving the greatest activity.

Response to Inactive Periods

____ 1. I stare, doodle, find something to watch.

____ 2. I hum or talk to others or myself.

____ 3. I find reasons to move, swing my feet, thump my desk, crack my knuckles, etc.

Response to New Situations

____ 1. I look around and/or examine structure.

____ 2. I talk about the situation, its pros/cons and what to do.

____ 3. I try out things; I touch them, manipulate them, try to find out how they work.

Emotionality

____ 1. I am somewhat repressed. I stare when angry, cry easily, beam when happy. My face usually reveals how I feel.

____ 2. I shout with joy or anger. I blow up verbally but soon calm down. I express my emotions verbally through changes in tone, volume, and/or pitch of my voice.

____ 3. I jump for joy and hug, tug, and pull when happy. When I'm angry, I stamp, jump, pound, and/or stomp off. My body reveals my emotions.

Communication

____ 1. I am quiet; I never really talk at length and get impatient when others do. I use words clumsily at times and use words like "look" and "see" frequently.

____ 2. I enjoy listening but cannot wait to talk sometimes. I like to hear myself and others talk. I use words like "listen" and "hear" frequently.

____ 3. I gesture when speaking. I talk with my hands. I stand or sit close when speaking or listening. I lose interest in detailed speech. I use words like "get," "take," and "do" frequently.

General Appearance

____ 1. I am neat and meticulous. I like order and choose not to vary my appearance much.

____ 2. Matching clothes is not important to me.

____ 3. I am neat, but because I am active, my clothes must be comfortable and move with my body.

Response to the Arts

____ 1. I am not particularly responsive to music; I prefer the visual arts, but I don't really talk about art. I can be deeply moved by visual displays like sunrises, sunsets, light displays. I see detail—individual shapes and colors—rather than the work as a whole.

____ 2. I like music more than visual art, but I can and do talk about what I see. Usually I appreciate the whole work rather than noticing details.

____ 3. I respond to music by physical movements: I prefer sculpture to painting. I like to touch statues and paintings both. I like exhibits which have things for me to do.

Answer Sheet

Circle the numbers below that correspond to your answers above.

Learning Style	1	2	3
Reading	1	2	3
Spelling	1	2	3
Handwriting	1	2	3

Memory	1	2	3
Distractibility	1	2	3
Problem Solving	1	2	3
Response to Inactive Periods	1	2	3
Response to New Situations	1	2	3
Emotionality	1	2	3
Communication	1	2	3
General Appearance	1	2	3
Response to the Arts	1	2	3

How to tell what kind of learner you are.

1. Add up your 1s, 2s, and 3s and record the totals below.

________	________	________	= 13 areas marked
1s Seeing	2s Hearing	3s Doing	

2. I learn primarily by ______________________.

Turn to the next page to find several examples of effective study methods for each learning preference (or style). These examples will help you as you begin to teach for all of the basic learning preferences—not just your own.

Examples of Effective Methods for Each Area of Strength

Seeing

Visual Learners

1. reviewing flashcards
2. seeing movies, filmstrips
3. reading the blackboard
4. examining diagrams and charts
5. looking at bulletin boards
6. reading
7. watching television
8. writing lecture notes and then reading them back
9. outlining and reading the outline
10. "seeing the situation in your head" (visualizing)

Hearing

Auditory Learners

1. listening to the teacher, film, filmstrip
2. taking notes and writing outlines, then reading them into a tape recorder and playing them back
3. reading notes out loud and listening to yourself as you read or having someone else read them to you

4. listening to others read as you follow along
5. saying the information you are trying to learn out loud
6. listening to pre-recorded tapes and records
7. listening to songs, television
8. playing the tape of your notes, etc. while you sleep

Doing

Kinesthetic Learners

1. drawing charts and diagrams of what you need to learn
2. writing many times what you need to learn
3. picturing yourself doing what you need to learn—example: picturing yourself as a member of the mob in Jerusalem that demanded that Pilate crucify Jesus
4. doing what you need to learn—example: as you are learning "ducere"—latin, "to lead"—taking your best friend (or whoever is available) and leading him/her to the kitchen, etc.
5. tinkering with the lawn mower engine, calculator, computer, basic math problem, etc.

Combination

Combination Learners

Pick learning methods from each chart and combine them when you study; make sure you choose more methods from your strong areas than from your weaker areas.

Example: Making flashcards and reading them out loud instead of just looking at them when you study. Writing each bit of information fifteen to twenty times; then saying the material on the flashcards again.

Example: Making flashcards and reading them aloud as you "lead your friend to the kitchen." Then reading the flashcards into a tape recorder and playing back the tape as you "lead your friend into the kitchen."

Example: Outlining together all lecture notes, reading notes, and study guides from one unit, and then recopying the outline several times, reading it out loud to yourself as you copy it.

Be creative in your combinations!

This learning-style checklist is drawn from a wide range of research that has been done in the area of learning preferences. While it is quite simple (compared to some of the inventories available), it will help you formulate a general idea of your own preferences.

Unless you scored all thirteen responses in one category, you will enjoy all these study methods to one degree or another, especially if your scores were very even, say 4-4-5 or 4-5-4. However, most people will score higher in one of the three areas than they do in the other two, 8-2-3 for example. That indicates you are strongest in that area and probably lean toward learning experiences in that category.

Let's say you did score 8-2-3. That means that you learn faster and better when there is a strong visual element. You may thoroughly enjoy sermons, and be moved by them, but you don't remember what the pastor said. Or, you had a drama class in college that was fun, but it was work. And you can't remember even one of the lines.

When you carry that preference into your own classroom, you also tend toward using learning experiences with a strong visual element because, from your memory, these are the best. For example, if you are an adult teacher you probably lecture a lot, simply because that has been the way adult teachers have operated for so long. You teach the way you were taught. But with your strong visual preference, you probably draw on the board, or distribute diagrams, or use an overhead projector. Or you wish you could do those things.

If you teach kindergarteners, you probably love the pictures that come along with the lessons. You like to look at them as much as the children do, and you use them in your stories.

But if your preference is "doing," then in that same class of five-year-olds you like to act out the stories with your body or your hands. You also use many objects the children can easily manipulate.

Know God . . .
Know Thyself

SEEING, HEARING, and DOING are three very simple categories that help us understand ourselves and our learning preferences.

These three categories also help us understand ourselves in that they give us insight into why we do the things we do in the classroom.

Couple an understanding of these three with a good perspective of your motivations for teaching in the first place, and you have a good foundation for growth as a teacher.

Remember teacher, after knowing God, "Know Thyself!"

"Mary, Mary, quite contrary,
 How can I help you grow?
Teach me awhile through my own learning style,
 And I'll grasp all the things I should know."

3

"The mediocre teacher tells,
the good teacher explains,
the superior teacher
demonstrates,
the great teacher inspires."
— Wm. Arthur Ward

Teachers Teach People, Not Information

"That checklist is amazing. It hit the nail right on the head for me." Joe was on the edge of his chair now, wide-eyed with the excitement of a new discovery. He could have continued the conversation into the wee hours. "I have to confess: When you told me that we teach the way we were taught, I didn't really understand. But this makes good sense.

Which Teaching Style Do You Use?

"As I think about it, I do use the kind of teaching style that I like the best. I guess I pretty much ignore the others because they don't appeal to me. But tell me how I can use this with my Junior boys."

Sally cleared her throat. It caught Joe's attention. His eyes moved her way only to be met by a stern glance, followed by the deliberate movement of head and arm that signifies the checking of the time. Enough said.

Betty and Dave caught it, too. Dave sank back in his chair and raised an empty coffee cup to his lips to cover the big smile that suddenly appeared. Betty spoke up, "I'm afraid if we tackled that one, we'd be here all night, and I know you're paying a babysitter. Let me just get you started thinking about it by asking Sally a question."

She turned to Sally. "Think back to all the teachers in church and school that you had when you were growing up." Betty paused. "Now tell me which one had the most influence on you."

Who Influenced Your Life?

While Sally is considering Betty's question, take time to do the same. In the space below, write the name of the teacher who most influenced your life. Then give the reasons why this particular teacher was so influential.

The teacher that influenced me most ___________________

What was it about that person that was so influential?

____

____

____

Sally didn't even stop to think. "That's easy. All this talk about teaching the way you're taught has had me thinking about Mrs. Bowman. She was my school teacher in the fifth grade. I don't remember anything specifically that I learned from her. I just remember doing different things in her class. I remember more of the things we did in her class than any other."

Betty asked, "Why does Mrs. Bowman stand out in your mind?"

How Did They Care for You?

"Because she cared about me. I just knew that she loved me, and she wanted me to enjoy learning as much as she did. As I think about it, she didn't treat me any differently from the rest of her students. I just knew she cared. In fact, I'll bet everyone in the class felt the same way."

"Were you more cooperative in Mrs. Bowman's classroom than you were in others?"

"Well, I generally was cooperative in school, but I would have done anything Mrs. Bowman asked me to do."

"What if Mrs. Bowman had shown you that attention but hadn't directed you in meaningful learning activities. Would you still remember her as the most influential?"

"Sure I would. That wouldn't change anyth . . ." Sally stopped in mid-thought. "Or would it? I see what you're suggesting. Her love and affirmation motivated me to get involved in learning activities. If she had been just another grandmotherly figure who didn't challenge and guide us, she wouldn't have had nearly the influence on me as I was growing."

Teachers Teach People, Not Information

"Exactly! To put it in an easy-to-remember phrase, TEACHERS TEACH PEOPLE, NOT INFORMATION. God didn't call us to be dispensers of facts, even facts about the most important message in all of history. He called teachers to be loving shepherds who feed His flock, workers who care deeply about each individual sheep.

"Some teachers act more like cattlemen than they do shepherds. Herd the sheep in on Sunday morning, fill the feeders with Bible stories, activities, discussion groups or the like, then send them back out.

"The shepherd, on the other hand, knows every sheep and cares for each one, individually." Betty was on her soapbox.

She continued, "Joe, now you answer one. As an adult, which teacher has had the most influence on you?"

"You mean which teacher I've had as an adult?" Joe asked.

"Yes."

"It would have to be Merrill Jones. I told you that I was willing to take this class of boys. But I had to pray about it a while because I hated to leave Merrill's class. I felt like I was really growing under his teaching."

"Why do you think Merrill's teaching is more influential than others?" Betty quizzed.

"He knows so much!"

"But does he just open the floodgates and let the information pour?"

A Teacher Is a Guide

"No," Joe said thoughtfully. He drew out the "o" as his brow furrowed, and he looked up into space. "No," he repeated. "Now that you mention it, he doesn't just dump a lot of knowledge on us. He wants us to grapple with the truth of God's Word and explore its implications for ourselves. He's more of an authoritative guide than he is a 'teacher' in the traditional sense."

"Sort of like a loving shepherd who guides God's sheep into a pasture and watches over them as they graze?" Betty was beaming a big smile. She knew she had hit home.

It was infectious. "I see!" said Joe. "All along I've been trying to get my guys into a lot of facts about the Bible, thinking that if they had enough information, their lives would be changed. But you're saying that we are to TEACH PEOPLE, NOT INFORMATION." Joe paused and looked up thoughtfully as his voice trailed off to nowhere, "Like a shepherd feeding sheep . . ."

A Teacher Is a Shepherd

Dave had been quiet as long as he could stand it. "Can I throw in an example? I always have to boil it down to something I know.

"Back to that football game. During the long weeks and months of practice, the coach is constantly teaching his players about the game of football, but he doesn't have them file into a classroom and lecture them on the finer points of the game. His teaching guides them to play the game better.

"And he knows every player on his team, what they do well and what they do poorly. He expects them to fit into his program, but he tailors his coaching to the team he has that particular year. He doesn't teach football to a group of boys. He teaches a group of boys how to play football. There's a big difference."

"TEACHERS TEACH PEOPLE, NOT INFORMATION," Joe repeated. "That puts the whole task in a completely different light. I'm excited. I can't wait to get back with my boys."

"That's the 'vision' we talked about earlier," Betty added. "'Duty' is carrying out impersonal tasks that the institution requires. 'Vision' is seeing what God is doing in people."

Reader, is the light dawning in your heart the way it has in Joe's? Take a few minutes to reflect on your attitude toward the issue of feeding God's sheep. Rate yourself by placing an "X" on the following scale.

How Do You Rate?

MY ATTITUDE TOWARDS GOD'S SHEEP (whatever age level I teach) HAS BEEN LIKE A:

CATTLEMAN									SHEPHERD
1	2	3	4	5	6	7	8	9	10

Now test yourself to see how well you know the sheep in your charge. On the next page, list the learners in your class in the space provided. Then, write something unique about each person. Finally, stop and pray for each one focusing on some specific need, concern, praise, etc.

NAME: S/HE IS UNIQUE BECAUSE:

1.

2.

3.

4.

5.

6.

7.

The concern that a shepherd has is one that extends past the feeding hour. Make thinking about and praying for your class members a habit—a labor of love.

Know Your Learners

"Joe, I'm enjoying this as much as you are, but we don't want to wear out our welcome." Sally gently tugged him back to earth.

"You're right, Sally. Besides, I don't know if I could take in anymore ideas." Turning to Dave and Betty he continued, "You two have opened a whole new world to me, one that I only dreamed could exist. How can I thank you?"

"No thanks necessary," Betty said graciously. "But, Sally, may I have two more minutes?"

"Sure." She didn't really want to end the conversation either.

"I think you've got the idea firmly in hand: KNOW YOURSELF and KNOW YOUR LEARNERS. I'm sure you will give each of those Junior boys a lot of personal attention. But one further idea will help even more. Let me introduce it with a question: You are different now than you were as a Junior boy, aren't you, Joe?"

"I'm not sure sometimes," Sally injected. Her comment brought the laughter she had hoped for.

"Well, in spite of having an unappreciative wife, I am different now." Joe enjoyed the ribbing.

"But you're the same person," Betty said. "The same person, but different. That is because God designed people to move through different life stages as long as they live. Junior boys are different from middle-school boys, my young single adults are different from senior citizens.

Learn the General Characteristics of the Age-level You Teach

"Knowing your boys will be easier if you know something about Junior boys in general—their interests, their attitudes, their problems. They all tend to be in a similar category. If you learn more about these shared traits, then knowing the individuals becomes easier and more meaningful."

"Where can I get this information?"

"She thought you'd never ask!" Dave said. Husbands are sometimes as irreverent as wives.

"I have a brief description of those characteristics in my file. Let me get it for you." Betty retrieved the two-columned paper for Joe. "Take it home with you and read over the various categories, then we'll talk again. Remember, God wants shepherds, not cattlemen."

That made everybody happy.

Sally broke up the gathering by standing and dropping her coat unceremoniously into Joe's lap. "Honey, could you help me with my coat?" She normally put her coat on herself, but this was a proven technique to get Joe back to earth.

The handshakes were genuinely warm, and the "thank yous" deeply felt.

Joe and Sally talked excitedly in the car on the way home. They sensed that they had just passed a milestone in their lives that would impact their service to God in a very positive way.

Be a Good Shepherd

Reader, Betty is right! Effective teachers know and love the individuals that make up their classes, and they know about the life characteristics these same people share. We've already asked you to think about your individual "sheep." Now, take a minute to familiarize yourself with the shared traits of the age level you teach.

Following is the chart Betty handed Joe from her file as they broke up their evening of discussion. It is adapted from the chart on pages 36 and 37 in the book *Superintend with Success* by Guy Leavitt (Standard). It is one of many charts available today that gives information about developmental levels of learners.

Locate the section that refers to the age level with which you work, then read through the characteristics. As you read each category, think about your "sheep." Compare them at their stage of development with the traits listed. Read the appropriate section with one of your learners specifically in mind. Can you see connections? Can you see opportunities to focus your teaching of the Bible? Can you see reasons why they respond in class the way they do?

Period in Life	General Characteristics	
I. EARLY CHILDHOOD		**Early Childhood Division**
A. Crib Baby (Birth to 12 months)	Key Word: Dependent Physical—requires a great deal of sleep, cries to communicate Mental—starting to learn through all five senses Spiritual—absorbs attitudes of attendants, saying very simple words	
B. Toddler (12-24 months)	Key Word: Discovery Physical—active, growing rapidly Mental—sees everything, wants to handle Spiritual—all s/he does is determined by others	
C. 2's and 3's	Key Word: Imitation Physical—active, leisurely, "me do it" Mental—realistic, inquisitive, likes "touch and feel" Spiritual—likes regular prayer before meals and bedtime, meaning of "thank you, God" is clearer	
D. 4's and 5's	Key Word: Receptivity Physical—continual motion, restless, wiggler Mental—open mind, a bundle of questions Spiritual—credulous, trusting, literal	
II. CHILDHOOD		**Children's Division**
A. Primary (Grades 1 and 2)	Key Word: Activity Physical—active, play is important	

		Mental—curious, imaginative, wants certainty Spiritual—discerning, capacity for reverence
	B. Middler (Grades 3 and 4)	Key Word: Involvement Physical—growth is more steady, coordination better, loves to participate Mental—likes learning games, likes to feel s/he belongs, is influenced by group approval Spiritual—coming to an understanding that s/he needs to make choices and decisions based on right and wrong
	C. Junior (Grades 5 and 6)	Key Word: Energy Physical—unbounded energy, loud, boisterous, thoughtless Mental—retentive memory, hero worshiper, inquisitive Spiritual—worshiper, "doer of the Word"
Youth Division	III. TEEN	
	A. Young Teen (Grades 7, 8, and 9)	Key Word: Transition Physical—rapid change, awkward Mental—critical, self-reliant, self-important, emotional Spiritual—religious awakening, faith yielding to reason, "Why, why!"
	B. Youth (Grades 10, 11, and 12)	Key Word: Aspiration Physical—loves achievement, emerging into manhood and womanhood Mental—radical, extreme, doubting Spiritual—unstable, age of decisions

IV. ADULT

A. Young Adult (18-24 years)	Key Word: Self-assurance Physical—mature Mental—real thinker, reason and judgment Spiritual—earnest seeking, sometimes scoffing
B. Early Maturity (25-34 years)	Key Word: Application A general getting down to business; definite tasks are begun and definite goals chosen
C. Full Maturity (35-64 years)	Key Word: Achievement Life is fully launched; each individual is himself or herself; a settled state
D. Late Maturity (65 and up)	Key Word: Meditation Physical decline; good, experienced judgment and knowledge; many adjustments such as facing death, loneliness, threat of being stereotyped; establishing satisfactory living arrangements (perhaps several times); desires to feel needed; possesses strong faith

This chart is a good overview of the stages through which people move in their development. (If you would like a more detailed explanation of the characteristics of each of these stages, see chapter three of a book by Guy Leavitt and Eleanor Daniel titled *Teach With Success,* also by Standard.) As you work closely with your learners from week to week, be sensitive to them as individuals. Allow this insight into their stage of development to increase your sensitivity to them as individuals. It can help you know and understand them better. As a result, you will become a more effective teacher!

4

"A teacher affects eternity; no one can tell where his influence stops."
— Henry Adams

Reaching and Teaching People to Know God

Sunday morning was better! Joe went into his classroom with a new sense of purpose. Even though the lesson wasn't much different from the ones he had taught before, he was sure he noticed a difference in his "sheep." Were they more involved or was he just imagining things?

Teach for Involvement

In any case, he felt differently about the class. He was able to get involved with the boys, less tied to his notes. Even the impulse to cover all the information in his outline was not as strong as usual.

But something was bothering Joe. Betty had opened up a whole new world to him, but there was something they hadn't had time to discuss that troubled him like a little dark cloud in the clear sky of that new world.

After thinking about it most of Sunday afternoon and talking it over with Sally, he decided to tackle it. He called Betty on Monday morning and asked if she and Dave could drop by some evening that week. They agreed on Tuesday evening. "We'll bring the dessert," Betty offered.

"Not on your life," Joe barked. "If you come to my house, you eat my dessert, or I should say Sally's dessert."

Betty finally agreed. Besides, Sally was famous for the sweets she served her guests.

Take Time for Fellowship

Tuesday evening found the four of them relaxing in the Christophers' living room. It hardly seemed that a week had passed. In fact, the only differences in the scene were the room, the dessert, and Joe's strange mood. The surroundings and the Swiss-chocolate torte were pleasant changes. Joe's concern wasn't.

This time, Betty didn't let the conversation run its course. After Sally served the torte and poured the coffee, she put the issue on the table, too. "Joe, last week when we finished you seemed very excited. But when you called me yesterday, you seemed worried about something. Is that why you wanted us to come over?"

Joe didn't respond immediately. He looked up at Sally, who raised her eyebrows, turned her head, and gave him that "Well-what-are-you-waiting-for" look.

"Yes, it is, Betty. Thanks to both of you for being willing to get together on such short notice."

"We did have to have our appointment secretary call and cancel all the personal audiences we had approved." Dave just couldn't let an opening like that pass.

"Dave!" Betty said in that motherly tone wives use to reprove husbands.

"Just kidding, Joe. Please continue."

Making a Difference

"Well, it's about our conversation last week. You're right. I was excited. I felt like you opened a door to a new world. It even made a difference in my class this past Sunday. But something has bothered me since we talked last week."

"What's that?" Betty asked. Dave could hear the concern in her voice.

"It's hard to express . . ."

"Hard to express!" Sally interrupted. "What he means is, he's afraid of hurting your feelings. I told him that was nonsense, that you would want to discuss the issue."

"OK," Joe said. "Sally's right. I don't want to hurt your feelings or offend you in any way."

"Nothing you could say would hurt my feelings," Betty said in a reassuring tone. "We're friends. What's bothering you?"

"It's your comment about TEACHERS TEACHING PEOPLE, NOT INFORMATION. The more I thought about it, the more uncomfortable I became. I believe we have to teach the Bible, nothing else. If all we're concerned about are the students and their needs, then what will become of teaching the Bible? We'll end up teaching them about who-knows-what?"

"Is that all?" Betty exclaimed with relief.

"Don't you think that's enough?"

"Oh, I'm sorry, Joe. I didn't mean to make light of what you said. It is a genuine concern that we should discuss. It's just that . . ."

"It's just that she thought the problem was that last week's cheesecake gave you a stomachache. Criticize her ideas, but watch what you say about her desserts." Dave was in a light-hearted mood.

That helped. The furrow left Joe's brow as he smiled.

"Joe, I'm impressed that you've thought through this thing so thoroughly," Betty continued, a smile on her face. "Last week we talked about the 'Who' of teaching—you and your learners. What we didn't get to was the 'Why.'"

"Isn't the 'Why' because God wants us to teach the Bible?" Joe looked puzzled now.

How Do We Teach the Bible?

"Certainly it is! But the thing that has you troubled is how the Bible is to be used in a people-centered setting, the best way to get God's eternal message across. But to answer that we have to get to the even deeper issue of 'Why.'

"Bear with me for a couple of minutes while we think back to the question of 'Why,'" Betty continued. "The popular view, among people who don't think through these issues from a teacher's point of view, is that Sunday school should be Bible-centered. They mistakenly believe that they are patterning their ministry after the ministry of Jesus."

"That's exactly how I feel. Are you telling me that Jesus' ministry was not Bible-centered?" Joe asked.

"Jesus' ministry was based on God's Word and full of God's Word, but it was people-centered. He used the Bible to help people know God. He was not concerned that they gain an encyclopedic knowledge of the Scripture."

Sally's eyes lit up as she interjected, "You know, I recall learning recently about the Pharisees back in Jesus' time. It seems they were so obsessed with teaching and interpreting God's law to and with each other that they had little if any interest in people. Isn't that one of the reasons Jesus questioned them so often?"

Be People-centered

"Yes!" Betty said. "They were the Bible-centered people of Jesus' world, and because they worried more about their Scripture than they did about people, God rejected them outright!"

"That really bothers me," Joe said. "It seems like you're saying that God's Word is not important."

"Hold on, Joe," Dave interruped. "Betty didn't say anything that doesn't reflect her deep commitment and love for the Scripture or anything that would indicate that she doesn't believe it as God's inspired Word from cover to cover."

"But to say that Jesus' ministry was not Bible-centered seems like heresy." Joe was struggling.

Dave continued, "She said that Jesus' ministry was based on the Bible and full of the Bible, yet people-centered. Remember, He Himself said that 'God so loved the world, that he gave his only begotten Son,' not, 'God so loved the Bible, that he sent his Son to teach it.' God gave His Word so we could know Him and introduce Him to others, not so we could become little Pharisees."

Joe had been listening intently. "Does the pastor know you feel this way?"

"Absolutely! Who do you think helped us understand this?" Dave's strength seemed reassuring.

"Joe, let me put it another way," Betty continued. "The issue is not whether we should teach the Bible or something else. In my twenty-plus years of teaching, God's Word is all I've taught. The real question is, 'How do we best use it to teach people?' And that's where the problems arise. You see, until recently you've been on the receiving end of teaching. From a learner's perspective, the Bible is always the authority; so your attitude naturally is that your classes have been Bible-centered. But that's the view from the pew."

"I like that," Dave said.

"Me, too," Sally added.

Why Do We Teach?

"Actually," Betty continued, "there is a question even more fundamental than how we use the Bible, and it's a question every teacher must ask. The answer will have a profound influence on your thinking and on your teaching. That question is, 'Why do we teach in the first place?'"

Reader: Take a minute to answer Betty's question. Be careful though. The answer is so simple that people often miss it.

We teach because: ____

"That's easy," said Joe. "We teach because Jesus told us to in the Great Commission."

"You're right," Betty responded. "We teach because we want to obey God. Your willingness to do that already has had an important influence on your Junior boys. But are there other reasons that motivated you to agree to take on your class?"

Reader: Stop and answer Betty's question from your own experience.

What other reasons do I have for teaching?

1. Jesus commanded us to teach! **Matthew 28:19, 20**

2. ____

3. ____

4. ____

After a few quiet moments of thought, Joe answered Betty's question, "For one, the Bible has had a profound impact on my life. I want to share that with people."

"Any others?"

"Yes. I care about people, especially these boys in elementary school. I remember how tough adolescence was for me. They will face so much. I want to help guide them toward the Lord, and the Bible will certainly help them."

Betty looked at Dave and Sally and said, "Joe, you just gave yourself away, and there are two witnesses!"

"Huh?" Joe's face took on a questioning look.

"First, you answered my question about why you want to teach. Those were reasons from your perspective. Then, the last thing you said answered my next question before I even asked it."

Joe was confused.

Betty continued, "That next question is, 'Why do you think God wants us to teach? What was behind the Great Commission?'"

Sally saw an opportunity to join the conversation and jumped in, "Because He loves the world and WANTS PEOPLE TO KNOW HIM. Christians who already know Him should be helping others get to know Him or get to know Him better."

"That's right," Betty exclaimed. "And what difference will knowing God make in their lives?"

"A lot!" Joe was back in the conversation. "They will be different people. They'll think differently and act differently . . ."

"And feel differently," Sally added.

"Exactly," Betty said as she took over again. "When people know God and grow in that relationship, their lives will be changed. That's what you said about your boys. You said that you wanted to guide them to the Lord, and that the Bible would help. You did not say you wanted to guide them to the Bible and the Lord would help."

Reaching and Teaching People To Know God

She was excited now. "God wants us to REACH people, then TEACH people with one aim in mind: SO THEY WILL KNOW HIM. And as people know God, they will be different. Their lives will change."

"You're right," Joe said. "I want my boys to know the Bible and to be strong in the Lord as they enter adolescence. But deep down my real desire is for them to know Jesus the way I do. Then they'll want to know the Bible and will have Him to help them be strong."

"Betty," Sally said, "put that into one of your little phrases for me."

"How about, REACHING AND TEACHING PEOPLE TO KNOW GOD."

Losing Our Vision

Reader: The Sunday school has undergone profound changes in the past eighty years, changes which have contributed to a general loss of the vision for REACHING AND TEACHING PEOPLE TO KNOW GOD. In their excellent book, *GROWTH—a New Vision for the Sunday School,* Win and Charles Arn and Donald McGavran point out the serious negative impact of these changes in terms of dramatic losses in the numbers of people involved in Bible study through the Sunday school in most churches. They also identify five reasons why this change has taken place.

Read through this list of four of their five reasons, then rank them "1," "2," "3," or "4" in terms of the negative influence each has had on the ministry of reaching and teaching people to know God. In other words, which of these four has done the most damage, which would be next, etc.

Priority Ranking

____ A. The focus of the Sunday school changed from those "outside" to those "inside." Sunday-school conventions, teacher-training programs, curriculum material all began to focus attention on the "Hows" of teaching, while the "Whys" of teaching became more obscure. The result was a decreasing interest in outreach and an increasing interest in nurture. . . . Internal concerns became a preoccupation, capsizing the delicate balance of ministry to the body and ministry through the body.

____ B. Leadership of the Sunday school shifted from the laity to professionals. There was less involvement by the many, and more involvement by the few. . . . Lay people were no longer the generals in the Sunday school, but became the foot soldiers.

____ C. A separation of roles evolved in the Sunday school and church. The EVANGELIST became the zealous, uncompromising charismatic leader whose message was to repent and be saved. Evangelism was what he did during a special crusade. The RELIGIOUS EDUCATOR became the thoughtful, quiet planner whose message was "let us grow spiritually." His concern was spiritual nurture. Bringing Christians to spiritual maturity was his major objective. Consequently, he had little time or concern for evangelism. The LAITY became those who participated in activities planned for them. They filled the chairs and watched the events. Except to serve on committees, usually focused on internal concerns of the church, roles of the laity were passive.

____ D. There developed a loss of community and sense of belonqinq. The neighborhood church became the drive-in church. Adults began to live in two worlds, Sunday and the rest of the week. Because of this, person-to-person relationships became less meaningful, resulting in the decline of a caring fellowship. The Sunday school seldom acted deliberately to counter this erosion of relationships, and the element of caring which once characterized the church and Sunday school declined.

As a result, in most churches, Sunday school became less and less a priority.

"I never stopped to think about that," Joe said. "It's terrible! How could we let those things happen to us?"

"But it's true!" Sally was disturbed. "I've felt for a long time that I'm more like a member of a special interest club than I am a disciple of Jesus Christ. I feel that I am turned inward. I feel like a spectator. I feel like I've lost the sense of belonging."

Betty looked at her friends with satisfaction. They were struggling with important questions. She knew that they were the kind of people who would be part of a solution. She wanted to encourage them with practical help, not be just another know-it-all who has keen insights into all the problems.

"This is a good news/bad news situation," she said. "That's the bad news. The good news is that in spite of these trends in the church and society, God still uses people like you and me to make a difference. Faithful lay people who love Jesus are leading others to Christ through the Sunday school and are helping believers know Him better."

"But what is it that these people have?" Sally asked.

Keep Your Main Task in View

"It's very simple. They know exactly why they are doing what they're doing, and keep that purpose in view at all times. That way, everything they learn about teaching (the 'Who,' the 'What,' the 'How,' and all the rest) helps them accomplish their goal. If they don't keep their purpose in mind, they end up shifting their focus from the 'Why' to the 'How,' just like the inward-focused Sunday school I read to you about."

"You mean they are so wrapped up in the process that they forget the product?" Joe asked.

"Yes," Betty responded.

"I've known engineers like that," Joe said.

"May I toss out an illustration?" Dave interjected. "You can talk about ideas only so long. Then you need a story."

"I agree," Sally chimed in. "Tell one, Dave."

Dave picked up Sally's enthusiasm and forged ahead. "There's a story about a famous female swimmer who was going to attempt to swim a channel. She trained for months so she could swim miles through the rough, cold, choppy water of the channel.

"The big day finally arrived. She, her coach, and her support team headed for the shore early in the morning. They covered her body with a thick layer of grease to protect her from the danger of hypothermia posed by the cold water. In a dense fog, they launched the escort boat while the swimmer slipped into the icy chop.

"Mile after mile, hour after hour, the woman knifed forward through the rough water. All the time she was only able to see a few yards ahead because of the fog. But hour after hour her strength slowly drained away. She had trained for it, was ready for it, but her strength was waning.

"Her coach leaned over the side of the escort boat to cheer her on. 'You can do it. Focus your strength. Just one more stroke. One more stroke. One more stroke.'

"But the cold and the fog and the pain and the frustration finally got her. She stopped swimming and in tears cried to be pulled into the boat. The coach wrapped her in blankets, then put his arms around her to help warm and reassure her as the boat sped toward the shore.

"The fog was so thick that even the skipper was surprised when they came in view of land only ninety seconds later. Our heroine had stopped swimming only a few hundred yards short of her goal. In a frustration only intensely committed people know, she gritted her teeth and shouted, 'If only I could have seen my goal! A few hundred yards would have been nothing!'

"This champion athlete was not defeated by the cold or the pain. She had trained and prepared for that. She was defeated," Dave spoke these last words slowly and dramatically to make sure his point was clear, "She was defeated because the fog prevented her from seeing her goal."

"Oh, how sad," Sally said. "She must have felt terrible."

Never Lose Sight of the Goal

"It is sad, but I think the light is beginning to dawn on me," Joe said thoughtfully. "Let me put together what you said last week and what you just told me to see if I am beginning to understand." He looked away from his wife and friends as if he were staring through the ceiling, then slowly said, "You're telling me that our job as teachers is not to teach the Bible, but to REACH AND TEACH PEOPLE TO KNOW GOD using the Bible. That's our goal, and we should never lose sight of it, even when the fogs of frustration or excitement come." He lowered his eyes. "And that's why we have to be people-centered, but still Bible-based. Right?"

Betty was ecstatic. "Yes! Yes, Joe. I couldn't have said it better myself. With that clearly in mind and our goal clearly in sight, then we will be protected from the inherent danger of becoming more concerned with the 'How' of teaching than with the 'Why.'"

"Eureka!" Dave boomed. "That calls for another cup of coffee."

5

"The Word of God is alive and powerful . . ."
— Hebrews 4:12

The Content of Our Teaching Is the Bible

And more coffee there was! Dave, being the ever-polite guest, also allowed Sally to give him a second piece of the torte. Even though the others abstained, he was willing to suffer for etiquette's sake.

The Bible Is the Source

During the lull in their discussion, Joe said enough to clue Dave and Betty to the fact that even though he seemed to be understanding everything, he still felt that the Bible was not getting its fair place. While their hosts were in the kitchen, Dave and Betty had a quick conference. They agreed to suggest that the foursome call Pastor Thompson and to make it a fivesome for a half hour or so, to see if he could help Joe work through his concern.

Joe and Sally returned, heard the proposal, and thought it was a great idea, as long as it didn't impose on their pastor. Dave assured them that Jim Thompson would tell them if there was a problem, and Betty called.

"He'd love to come over," Betty reported. "Jane and the children are at the mall."

The group settled back, sipped their coffee, and let Dave entertain them with another of his stories. He had barely delivered the punch line when a knock came at the door.

"That must be Jim," Joe said, as he stood up and headed for the door. "I'm glad he waited long enough to miss that punch line. I hate to see grown men groan!"

"Ooooh!" the other three responded in unison as Joe welcomed the pastor.

Jim Thompson was a tall man of about forty. He began adult life as a school teacher. During summer vacations he took a job selling insurance. One night as he sat in a client's living room discussing life insurance, the talk turned to death and dying. By the end of the discussion, Jim sold the policy, but his client also led him to the Lord.

His discovery of new life in Jesus changed him so completely that he sensed God's call to the ministry. He enrolled in seminary and let the insurance business support him. The unique part of the story is Jim's unusual blend of a pastor's heart with an educator's training.

As Jim entered the room, cordial greetings were exchanged, as well as good-natured barbs about who tells the worst jokes. Finally, Betty jumped in and brought him up to date on their conversations of the past two weeks.

He listened attentively, asked a couple of questions, then requested that Joe express his concern in his own words.

Joe felt on the spot. While he wanted to talk about the issue, he didn't want to sound like he was criticizing Dave and Betty. But he swallowed his self-consciousness and began. "Pastor, it's like this. I hear Betty and Dave giving me what I think is very good advice. I like what I hear. It has given me hope and encouragement as I think about teaching my class.

The Message Must Be Clear

"But I'm still bothered by my concern as to where the Bible fits. I don't want to be narrow-minded, but I don't want to lessen my commitment to the Scripture by one iota. Phrases like TEACHERS TEACH PEOPLE, NOT INFORMATION and REACHING AND TEACHING PEOPLE TO KNOW GOD, sound full of wisdom, but I know that even bad ideas come to us dressed up like good ones. I want to be sure that whatever philosophy I adopt, the Bible has its rightful place. Can you help me think through this?"

"I think I can," Jim Thompson said. "It is a struggle that I am familiar with because I've had it so many times. First, let me assure you that the advice Dave and Betty gave you is sound. The phrases you used and the explanation Betty made point to the issues that lie at the very heart of Christian education. We are, quite simply, in the people business.

Philosophy Is Important

"Let me also assure you that every thoughtful person who is committed to the Bible and who has been engaged in Sunday school or another Bible-teaching ministry has had the same mental struggle you are going through now. If God had called us to teach the Bible, then our worries would be over. We would just gather people in a room and begin to teach.

"But because God called us to make disciples, and because the Bible is our primary tool in that process, we have to think about with the way we use the Bible to make disciples. In other words, we have to ask 'What is the message we want to get across?'"

Joe was looking perplexed. "I'm still not clear."

We Use the Bible To Change Lives

"I think I understand," Sally said. "See if I'm right. We are," she stopped and rephrased her statement, "I mean teachers are to TEACH PEOPLE, NOT INFORMATION, but the subject matter is always the Bible. The way we use the Bible might change from class to class or from one age group to another, but the 'What' of teaching always is the Bible."

Betty had been quiet intentionally. She didn't want to cause confusion. But she did ask a question hoping Pastor Thompson would expound on it. "Jim, would you explain to us the different approaches people take for studying the Bible in classes?"

"Sure. I'd be glad to. Think about the Bible studies you have been involved in over your lifetimes. Sometimes you memorized verses, or the ten commandments, or the books of the Bible. Other times you read a passage and discussed how it applied to your lives. Or you studied what the Bible has to say about a specific topic; say family life. Those are all different ways of studying God's Word."

"But isn't just plain studying the Bible the best approach?" Joe asked.

"Joe, everyone thinks that his or her approach is 'just plain studying the Bible.' And in a sense they're right. The Bible is always used, but in different ways."

"That's what I mean," Joe countered. "If you become people-centered instead of Bible-centered, then who knows where you will end? Sooner or later you'll come to a place where anything goes. I don't think that is pleasing to God."

Dave stirred again in his chair long enough to ask Joe, "Just what do you mean by 'just plain studying the Bible?'"

"I mean taking a passage of Scripture and learning what God has to say to us from it."

There Is More Than One Way To Study the Bible

"But, Joe, that's not the only way you study the Bible," Pastor Thompson said.

"Yes it is, or at least, I think it is."

Jim Thompson continued, "Do you remember the men's retreat last fall, the one about being a better husband and father?"

The pastor waited as Joe nodded in the affirmative. "Did we study the Bible?"

Another affirmative nod.

"I mean did we 'just plain study the Bible?'"

"Well, no. Not in the way I just described. But we did study the Bible. I left the lodge feeling I knew what God expected of me in my own family responsibilities for the first time in my life." As Joe spoke that last sentence a smile slowly crept across his face. "I see what you're saying. I didn't come away from that retreat as an expert on what God says about family life, but I did come away equipped to be a better husband and father because of what I learned about God and His perspective."

"I think he's got it!" Dave's attempt at a British accent was funnier than the timing of the remark.

"I think so, too," Pastor Thompson said. "Joe, it is true that our job is to REACH AND TEACH PEOPLE TO KNOW GOD. But right underneath that is the bottom line on what we teach those people. THE CONTENT OF OUR TEACHING IS THE BIBLE. The question with which a teacher always must struggle is, 'What is the best way to use the Bible with the people God has given me to teach?'"

"Then how do we answer that question, pastor?" Joe asked with a transparent sincerity.

"Yes," Betty said, "how do we answer it? Maybe I'm not too clear on this and that's why I confused Joe."

"If teaching the Bible is a given, then the question is, 'What is our objective in teaching the Bible?' In other words, what do we hope to accomplish?"

"I thought we had already agreed that our objective was REACHING AND TEACHING PEOPLE TO KNOW GOD." Joe looked like he was getting confused again.

"By all means," Jim said. "It is. But your objectives have to be specific. You have to ask what specific material you will teach and how you will teach it in order to reach your overall objective of helping people know God."

Joe stopped him again, "You mean as an engineer, my overall

objective is to construct a bridge, but I have to decide the best materials and construction techniques for that particular job."

"Yes, that is precisely what I mean. And in Christian education, there are four basic approaches to determining what materials and techniques are the best, each one deriving their objectives from a different source.

Back To the Bible

"The first approach is the one you obviously have, Joe. I call it the 'Back to the Bible' approach. People who hold this view see the immense scope of the Word of God and believe that this body of divine communication should be the source of our objectives. These objectives, then, consist of the specific knowledge about the Bible and its story that should be imparted to students.

"The late J. Vernon McGee's 'Through the Bible' radio program is based on this approach. In a Sunday school, you'd see this approach expressed in the adult electives that focus on the study of individual Bible books; Romans for example."

"That is the way I think it should be done," Joe said. "If we can just get people knowing God's Word well enough, then things will go much better for them."

Passing On the Faith

Jim continued undaunted, "I agree that this is an important approach, but it is not the only valid one. Be patient as I explain the others. I call the second approach 'Passing on the Faith.' This view sees the great, enduring values the Bible expresses as the source of our teaching objectives. These are the spiritual values that are transmitted from one generation of Christians to another. Paul called these enduring values 'the Faith.' The Bible is the basis for this approach, but detailed study of Bible content is not as important as transmitting these important values.

"Chuck Swindoll's radio program, 'Insight for Living' is built on this approach. He wants to help people deal with specific problems, but he is much more concerned with focusing on Biblical truth and values that serve as principles of faith, not detailing people's knowledge of the Bible story. In a Sunday-school setting, a class based on this approach might be 'A Biblical View of Sex,' or 'God's Plan for Families.'"

"Like the men's retreat last fall?" Dave asked.

"Like the men's retreat," repeated Jim. "Now Joe, does Chuck Swindoll teach the Bible?"

A cautiously affirmative nod.

"But not like J. Vernon McGee. Both point people to God's perspective embodied in the Scripture, but they do it in different ways. Do you fault Swindoll for not teaching the way McGee taught?"

"No. I see what you mean. What are the other approaches?"

"One more word on number two. This one is the basis for most curriculum for the Early Childhood and Children's Divisions. The little ones are not expected to learn many specifics about the Bible. Instead, the lessons introduce and reinforce the basics of God's ways. They learn the values and principles of the Bible so that as they mature they will have a firm foundation."

"I see!" Joe smiled. "This past Sunday my boys had a lesson from Daniel. It was the story in which Daniel and his friends refuse to eat the food from the king's table. The purpose of the lesson was not that the boys learn all the details of the story. Instead they were supposed to explore the idea of being faithful to God even when it's not easy."

"And that is a spiritual value communicated throughout the Bible," Dave added.

Preparing for Life in the World

"Well, on to the third approach. I call it, 'Preparing for Life in the World.' This is the approach used most often by Christian psychologists and sociologists. It sees the problems of contemporary society pressing in on people. Those problems then become the source from which learning objectives are derived. They seek to use the Bible to help people deal effectively with the problems they face as they live in the world.

"James Dobson's 'Focus on the Family' is this way. In each program, he tackles a specific problem from a psychologists perspective and applies the Bible's teaching to help people solve the problem. In a Sunday-school setting, a class for teens like 'Handling Peer Pressure' or, for adults, 'The Christian and AIDS' would be the kind of class this approach will foster.

Joe looked at Betty and Dave, "Like the lesson in the youth group that I questioned."

Meeting Individual Needs

"The last one," Jim continued, "is 'Meeting Individual Needs.' In this approach, the teacher considers the group of learners s/he is responsible for and compares what is known about them to a Biblical standard. The gap between the way they are and the way they should be is the need. The teacher chooses objectives that will help close the gap and meet this need.

"Billy Graham is a media example of this approach. He sees peoples' sinful condition, the way they are, and preaches specifically so that their sinful condition will change by meeting Jesus, thus moving them where they should be. In a Sunday-school setting, a class of middle-aged adults might agree to study a book on 'Knowing God in Mid-life,' or a teacher of teens might design a lesson on 'Building Relationships' because her class has been struggling in this area."

"Jim, I'm not sure of the difference between 'Meeting Individual Needs' and 'Preparing for Life in the World,'" Betty said. "They seem a lot alike to me."

"They are a lot alike," Jim responded. "The difference is that in the 'Meeting Individual Needs' approach, the objectives are derived from a specific need exhibited by the class. In the other, 'Preparing for Life in the World,' objectives are formulated based on the pressing problems presented by our society as a whole, not on specific issues the class is facing. Sometimes they look a lot alike."

When Jim finished, a thoughtful silence fell on the group. The foursome genuinely pondered his idea.

Joe broke the silence. He sounded overwhelmed as he said, "That sure makes sense, Jim. I guess I'm sitting here wondering which approach is the best."

A Well-rounded Program of Christian Education Uses Several Methods

"The answer to your question is that each of them is the best approach. Each one uses the Bible in a unique way to help people know God and His ways, but each approach meets people at different places in their lives. That's why Graham, McGee, Swindoll, and Dobson are so different yet so effective. That's also why a well-rounded Christian education program is so important to the life and health of the church. People of different ages and life situations can connect with God's Word in different ways and be edified all the more."

"Let me make one of my analogies here." Dave looked like he was about to burst. "On a football team, the football is the one thing they all have in common . . . "

"What about uniforms?" Sally had a mischievous look on her face as she interrupted Dave.

And he loved it. "I knew I liked you. Anyway, they all handle the ball, and they all want to get it past their goal line to score. But they all look at it differently. The center is a delivery boy, making sure the boss gets the package when he wants it. The quarterback sees it as an object to be managed. He has to get it to the right player at the right time. A split end looks at it as if it were a piece of air mail that he wants to get his hands on so he can run downfield. A tackler sees it in yet a different way. They all play the game sharing the same ball, each team trying to put points on the scoreboard, but their individual objectives are all very different."

Joe was dismayed. "Boy, if that's the case, then I am a rookie on the field all by myself. How in the world do I know which approach I should use and when?"

"That's where the Sunday-school team comes in, Joe," Betty said. "They decided on the curriculum we should use for the children and youth. As Jim said, those divisions use the 'Passing on the Faith' approach that is built into the curriculum. The adults and sometimes the youth choose a different approach to help round out their programs."

"And that's OK," Jim added, "because of their more complex needs."

"So I don't have to worry about choosing the best approach and building lessons on it?"

"Oh no, Joe!" Betty exclaimed. "That's why we have curriculum and a team. You should be aware of what is going on and keep yourself committed to the fact that THE CONTENT OF OUR TEACHING IS THE BIBLE. But as a team, we work together in training and planning so none of us is on the field by himself. Working together, we all score."

"Even if an individual teacher struggles once in a while." Dave's remark brought a series of nods and a sense of release. They all knew they had crossed the goal line together.

Which Approach Is Yours?

Check the approach to the Bible that best describes your view of the way we should select teaching/learning objectives.

____ 1. "Back to the Bible"—The Bible is our textbook and our goal should be to see that learners learn as much about it and what it says as possible. Then they will be equipped with specific Biblical promises and knowledge to handle any life situation.

Examples: J. Vernon McGee, and Bible book studies in Sunday school.

____ 2. "Passing on the Faith"—Our objectives should be to use the stories and teachings of the Bible to inculcate enduring spiritual values into our learners. That way they have principles to apply in any situation.

Examples: Chuck Swindoll, and most children and youth curriculum.

____ 3. "Preparing for Life in the World"—By identifying the pressing problems in our society, we derive teaching/learning objectives to help equip Christians with the Biblical perspective they need in order to deal with the problems.

Examples: James Dobson; the "Christian and AIDS" class.

____ 4. "Meeting Individual Needs"—By looking closely at our own class members, we see areas in which they need God's help (the way it is). We conceive objectives that will apply the Bible to meet those needs (and bring them to the way it should be).

Examples: Billy Graham, and in the Sunday school, a series of lessons on "Loving One Another" in a class full of dissension.

6

"For every person wishing to teach, there are thirty not wanting to learn."
— W. Sellar & R. Yeatman

A Bit of Hindsight

Before we rejoin our friends, let's look back to make sure that you have grasped the basic ideas we've covered so far. There are five of them:

Teachers Are Made, Not Born

Remember the two categories of teachers? One type teaches the way s/he was taught. This teacher operates almost entirely on the energy and know-how picked up while s/he was a student. The perspective gained as a class participant no more prepares a person to be a good teacher than playing in the high school band equips a person to be the conductor of an orchestra.

A teacher who builds his/her teaching "house" on that foundation ends up one of three ways: 1) quitting after a period of time because of the continual frustration, 2) perservering in the task because of his/her sense of duty and living with the frustration, or 3) making a conscious commitment, slowly developing into a teacher that falls into the other category.

That other category is full of the kind of teachers who are

MADE, NOT BORN. They begin teaching the way they were taught, but soon make a commitment to learn, stretch, grow, acquire new skills, observe, read, and otherwise do what it takes to become effective.

It is true that God has given some individuals the gift of teaching. They have an amazing ability to bring God's Word to life. These people are gifts from God to the church. But the church also needs many more believers, not specially gifted, to assume teaching roles. These are the people who grow into being good teachers.

Some might argue that only people with the gift of teaching should be teaching. But to say that is as ridiculous as saying the only people who should give are those to whom God has given the gift of giving. Or the only people who should be sharing Jesus with those who do not know Him are the individuals gifted for evangelism.

Some teachers are gifted individuals, given by God to the church. The majority are committed people like you and me who believe that TEACHERS ARE MADE, NOT BORN.

Teacher, Know Thyself

Once you realize that becoming an effective teacher is a process (MADE, NOT BORN), then the first order of business is to take a personal inventory. What is your commitment level? To what are you committed–Duty? Or a vision of what God can do in people's lives when they meet Him? Obviously, we want VISION so we can see what God is doing and participate with Him in His work.

Also, KNOW THYSELF means understanding your own learning and teaching preferences. You'll recall that we identified three:

- SEEING (visual)
- HEARING (auditory)
- DOING (kinesthetic)

You took a learning-styles inventory and now know which of those three you prefer. We hope you also realize that the learners in your class all have their own preferences, different from yours. By structuring experiences in your classroom that engage your learners in SEEING, HEARING, and DOING, you heighten the effectiveness of the learning activities (a chapter on the specifics of "how" to do this is coming up).

Teachers Teach People, Not Information

Once we realize we can grow as a teacher and then take our own personal inventory, our next step is to focus on the learner. Apart from the work of the Holy Spirit, this was the most powerful aspect of the ministry of Jesus–He was people-centered.

Remember, God called us to be shepherds, not cattlemen. We have to know the people in our care. We have to know their names, where they are in a relationship to the Lord, what their family lives are like, etc., etc. Otherwise we are only teaching information. Remember, Karl Marx knew the Bible very well. Bible information alone will not change lives.

In the process of knowing your individual learners, being sensitive to their stage of life will help you focus your teaching to maximize its impact. The chart and the mini-articles in chapter three are good reference points for you in the future.

Reaching and Teaching People To Know God

Why we teach was the next concept we tackled. Remember that Betty asked Joe to identify why he decided to teach. First he said that he volunteered to teach in order to obey God. The Great Commission commands it. Also, he likes to work with boys, especially Junior boys, so he can help them better adjust to adolescence.

But when Betty pressed him, the real reason came out. He wanted his boys to KNOW JESUS the way he did. They agreed that the purpose of teaching is not to change lives–that's the work of the Holy Spirit. Our goal is REACHING AND TEACHING PEOPLE TO KNOW GOD.

We reviewed Arn, McGavran, and Arn's 4 reasons the Sunday school has waned in effectiveness over the past century:

1. The focus of the Sunday school changed from those "outside" to those "inside."
2. Leadership of the Sunday school shifted from the laity to the professionals.
3. A separation of roles evolved, distinguishing "evangelist" from "educator" and both of those from "laity."
4. There was a loss of community and the sense of belonging.

Because of the vital importance of teaching to the fulfillment of the Great Commission, the teacher should always keep the WHY of teaching clearly in mind. The WHY has to be more important than the HOW, even though you can do without neither one. Dave's story of the swimmer illustrated this point–we have to keep our eyes on the goal: REACHING AND TEACHING PEOPLE TO KNOW GOD.

The Content of Our Teaching Is the Bible

Pastor Jim Thompson joined the group to help Joe work through the one problem that was plaguing him, i.e., what is the role of the Bible in Christian education. After allaying Joe's fear that if he was people-centered in his teaching he would eventually leave the rock-solid foundation of God's Word, Jim explained the four different approaches people use in teaching the Bible. Remember, they are different because each looks to a different source for teaching objectives.

1. BACK TO THE BIBLE– the Bible is our textbook, and our goal should be to see that learners learn as much about it and what it says as possible. That way, they will be equipped with specific Bible promises and knowledge to handle any life situation.

2. PASSING ON THE FAITH–our objectives should be to use the stories and teachings of the Bible to inculcate enduring spiritual values into our learners. That way they have principles to apply in any situation.

3. PREPARING FOR LIFE IN THE WORLD–by identifying the pressing problems in our society, we derive teaching/learning objectives to help equip Christians with the Biblical perspective they need in order to deal with the problems.

4. MEETING INDIVIDUAL NEEDS–by looking closely at the people in our own class, we see areas in which they need God's help (the way it is). We conceive objectives that will apply the Bible to meet those needs (and bring them to the way it should be).

A Summary

There they are, the foundation stones for your development as a teacher:

—TEACHERS ARE MADE, NOT BORN
(you can grow in your ability and effectiveness)

—KNOW THYSELF
(gain a vision and know your learning style)

—TEACHERS TEACH PEOPLE, NOT INFORMATION
(know your learners)

—REACHING AND TEACHING PEOPLE TO KNOW GOD
(our goal is people knowing GOD)

—THE CONTENT OF OUR TEACHING IS THE BIBLE
(and it is used different ways)

CONGRATULATIONS! You have a good handle on the basics. Now let's rejoin Joe and Betty as they make these ideas practical with some "how-tos." Dave would say, "Let the rubber meet the road."

7

"If the shoe fits,
you're not allowing
for growth."
— Robert N. Coons

People Learn Best When They Are Involved

" . . . and Father, guide us as we work on becoming better teachers and as we plan our sessions for the next month. We want You to use us in the lives of the children You've entrusted to us. In Jesus' name, amen."

A Regular Training/Planning Time Is Essential

Diane Thompson's "amen" was like an "all-clear" to the group of children's teachers gathered on this third Wednesday for their monthly training/planning meeting. In unison, coughs, squirms, the shuffling of papers, and the realigning of chairs indicated this team was ready to go to work.

The "team" is the teaching staff of the Children's Division at Joe and Sally's church. Diane is the leader of the Junior Department. The Primary and Middler departments join Diane's department each month for the first portion of the session. It is the only time they meet together as a division. Even though Joe had been teaching for three months, he hadn't attended any of the planning meetings. Oh, he had been invited.

Diane even had stressed how important the meetings were to the overall success of the Bible teaching. But he had been busy. And besides, that sort of thing always is for "them," not "me."

The real problem was that Joe had volunteered to do "jobs," even though he didn't call them that. He was careful to use more spiritual terminology, because he didn't want to belittle the tasks. But they were still jobs. Even the teaching responsibility with the Junior boys was a "job."

A "Job" or a "Calling"

But since his talks with Betty and Dave, he had come to realize that no matter what he called them, "jobs" could never be a "calling." The difference was vision.

Now he had a vision for REACHING AND TEACHING PEOPLE TO KNOW GOD. At last he understood the meaning and the value of teaching. Joe's teaching "job" had become a calling, and now he wanted to pick up as many specific "how-tos" as possible.

Betty fueled Joe's newfound fire with her encouragement. Before she and Dave left the Christopher's house that night, she gave Joe several examples of the importance of ongoing training and planning in any worthwhile task. True to form, Dave added a valuable tidbit. He gave Joe one more truth-in-a-nutshell phrase to guide him: GROWING NEVER STOPS, TRAINING NEVER ENDS.

As if that weren't enough, one more incentive arose out of their meetings. During all the discussions with the Spates and Jim Thompson, Sally's heart was stirred, too. She volunteered to work with Joe and the others in the Junior Department. However, before she assumed responsibilities, she wanted to observe the department in action for a month or so, and she wanted to attend a training/planning meeting. That was all the more reason for Joe to be there on that Wednesday night.

Unknown to Joe and Sally, Betty had made a point of contacting Diane just after the last discussion with the Christophers. She explained what had happened and asked Diane to spend the training portion of the upcoming meeting on Bible Learning Activities. She knew Joe and Sally would benefit from training in different learning methods because their enthusiasm was so fresh. Diane agreed.

Following Diane's prayer, several general announcements were made. Then it was time for the training period.

Diane walked to the overhead projector, switched it on, and read the hand-lettered words filling the screen:

People learn best when . . .

"How would you complete that statement?" Diane asked the group.

Write Your Response Here

Reader, how would you complete Diane's statement? Take a minute to think about it, then record your response in the margin. First impressions are usually pretty good ones, so write the first two or three ideas that come to your mind.

"When they are active in the class," Valda said as Diane wrote her response on the transparency.

"When they are concentrating," came another response.

"When they are interested in the topic."

"When there's lots to do."

"When they are excited about what they're learning."

"Lots to do. Excited." Diane mumbled as she wrote their responses on the transparency. She turned from the projector to the screen, looked admiringly and said, "That's a good list. Anything else?"

Hesitantly, like the newcomer he was, Joe said, "People learn best when what they're studying is relevant to their lives."

"Relevant." Diane wrote as she repeated Joe's contribution. "Those are all good completions to my statement, and they are all 'right on.' Thanks for sharing your ideas." She switched off the projector and put a different transparency down on the glass surface. "Would it be fair to say that all your responses could be summed up in this phrase?" She turned the projector back on, and the group saw:

PEOPLE LEARN BEST WHEN THEY ARE INVOLVED

How Do We Get Our Learners Involved In Bible Study?

Betty said, "That's a good summary. If people are busy in class, interested, discovering the Bible's relevance, or whatever, they are involved."

"I agree," someone else said. Nods of agreement could be seen all around the room.

"If it's true that PEOPLE LEARN BEST WHEN THEY ARE INVOLVED," Diane continued, "then one of the most important ongoing issues that we as teachers face is just how to get our learners involved and how to keep them involved."

"Amen!" one teacher said as the heads began to bob again.

Joe was nodding the affirmative and following the conversation like a spectator at a tennis match. He wanted to see their faces as the teachers made comments.

"The methods we use to get and keep that involvement are called Bible Learning Activities (BLAs for short)." Diane reinforced her point by projecting the three words on the screen. "Some of you are familiar with that terminology and this will be a review. To others though, this will be unfamiliar and what I say will be an introduction. In either case, talking about it as a group will put us all on the same ground.

What Is a Bible Learning Activity?

"Good involvement methods are first Bible Learning Activities," she said, emphasizing "Bible" with her voice and underlining it on the transparency. "Because our goal is REACHING AND TEACHING PEOPLE TO KNOW GOD, and because God has given us the Bible for that very reason, everything we do in the class must be based on the Bible. Activity for activity's sake—doing something simply because the kids might enjoy it or because it's a neat idea—simply is not appropriate. Everything we do must involve learners in exploring the Bible and discovering God's truth in a way they can apply to their lives."

That made Joe want to shrink in his chair. After all the fuss he had made about teaching the Bible with Betty, Dave, and Jim, he remembered the gimmick he had used to try to get his boys talking one recent Sunday morning. He was glad Sally didn't know about it, or he might be pulling her elbow out of his ribs.

Diane continued, "Good involvement methods are also Bible Learning Activities." She underlined the word "Learning" with a different colored pen. "The methods we use are tools to help us ensure that learning takes place in our classrooms. You know the old saying, 'You can lead a horse to water, but you can't make him drink.' Well, Bible Learning Activities are the tools we use to entice the horses to drink and to make sure that they have the best possible experience at the creek."

Three Kinds of Bible Learning Activities

Pat Humbles, the Primary Department leader spoke up, "Diane, I attended a teaching seminar recently and the speaker said, 'We must give three invitations to the learning party.' He meant that each Sunday, we should include learning activities that appeal to the three learning styles, seeing, hearing, and doing."

"That's a great way to think about it, Pat," Diane said. "Can you give us an example of what he meant?"

"If I know you," Pat responded, "you have planned something to demonstrate that very idea for children, so let me talk about how it applies to us as adults. And I'll use you as an example. We've been in this meeting fewer than ten minutes, but already you have us involved in all three levels. We're seeing because you are using the overhead projector as we talk about Bible Learning Activities; we're hearing by listening to what you and the others have to say; and we're doing because we are participating by giving our responses."

Learning, Not Babysitting, Is Our Aim

"Thanks, Pat. That means I've done my job. I've involved you in all three areas, and most of you didn't even realize it. But back to our second point," she said, pointing to the word "Learning" on the overhead again. "Learning, not babysitting, is the aim of all we do in class.

"Can you guess what the third characteristic of good methods might be?" she asked, as she underlined the third word—Activity. They all smiled. "You guessed it! We should engage people in Bible Learning Activities. If we all agree that PEOPLE LEARN BEST WHEN THEY ARE INVOLVED, then we have to put feet on that belief by getting them involved, and that means activity on their part."

"But, Diane, how can people learn if they're so busy doing a lot of different activities?" Joe had never been too self-conscious about asking questions, even when he was new to a group. "Doesn't all the busy-ness make the class too chaotic for real learning to occur?"

"Let me answer your question with a question, Joe," Diane said. "What have you learned so far in this training session?"

"That's easy. PEOPLE LEARN BEST WHEN THEY ARE INVOLVED, and teachers can involve students with Bible Learning Activities."

"Good, Joe. I couldn't have said it better myself. But you said that answering my question was easy. Would it have been that easy if I simply had stood before you and told you what you should know—no projector, no discussion, no questions, no visuals?"

"Well," he paused thoughtfully, "no, I guess it wouldn't have been so easy. When I think of the term, 'Bible Learning Activities,' I can see you underlining each of the three words with different colored pens."

"We're not studying the Bible right now, so using the projector is not a Bible Learning Activity," Diane responded, "but it is a Learning Activity. And it sounds to me like an effective one. Joe, what you're really concerned about is the chaotic effect of activities just for activity's sake. I would agree with you there. Our time with our learners is too short and too precious to waste it on busy work. But," she emphasized, "our time is also too precious to be wasting it on class plans that have good intentions but never engage people in real learning."

"You're right," Joe said. "The reason I'm here in the first place is because after three months of good intentions with my Junior boys, I was frustrated because I knew they weren't learning anything from me." Joe had never been self-conscious about admitting his own shortcomings to a group either.

"I think we all agree with Joe's summary of our session thus far," Diane said, as she included the whole group in her conversation with Joe. "PEOPLE LEARN BEST WHEN THEY ARE INVOLVED, and the best way to think about getting them involved is with Bible Learning Activities."

She continued, "I know you want to learn more about them and how they are used, especially how our curriculum uses them. I have a filmstrip on BLAs that will give us some great new insights."

"Seeing and hearing?" Joe asked with a smile.

"Seeing and hearing!" Diane repeated. "And in a few minutes you will be doing as well. I have two sample BLAs set up for us in the back of the room. You'll get to participate in one after the filmstrip."

"I knew it!" Pat said.

Diane just smiled. "Lights, please."

Who Learns Most in Your Class?

Reader: Everything we do in our classrooms, whether we teach babies or senior adults, is activity. Someone is doing something all the time. The question we as teachers must face is, "Who is active in my classroom—the learners, the teacher, or both?" If PEOPLE LEARN BEST WHEN THEY ARE INVOLVED, then it is our responsibility to involve them in the study of the Bible as best we can.

That's illustrated in this question, "Who learns the most in your class—you or your learners?" The answer of course is, "you!" That's because you are the one who is most involved. Spend the same energy planning how to involve your learners as you do planning your own involvement and the results will be incredible. Your students will cease being an audience for your Bible teaching show and become active partners in learning the Bible so they can grow in knowing God. But remember, they are only the participants, you are the guide. They can't participate if you don't plan for and encourage their involvement.

But obviously that involvement takes on different forms with different ages.

Early Childhood Division

These are God's smallest learners, the preschoolers in the Early Childhood Division. Because infants and toddlers (birth through twenty-four months) are in a category all by themselves, we don't have enough space in this brief introduction to treat their special learning needs adequately. If you are a teacher of these little ones, please see the following excellent books:

Caring for Babies by Joan Leach and Patricia St. Louis (Standard #14-03188)

Teaching Toddlers by Betty Aldridge, Kathy Downs, and Joy M. Grewell (Standard #14-03189)

Teaching Your Child About God: You Can't Begin Too Soon by Wes Haystead (Regal Books)

Seven Categories of BLAs for Preschoolers

Bible Learning Activities for two-to-five-year olds fall into seven broad categories:

- Family Living
- Blocks
- Nature
- Books
- Puzzles
- Music
- Art

As you think about planning meaningful Bible Learning Activities for the young child, remember two important characteristics. The first is that for the young child PLAYING AND LEARNING GO HAND-IN-HAND. Yes, they need structured time for singing, finger fun, and Bible stories, but they also need large doses of guided play time, with an adult talking and singing about the Bible truth in ways that relate it to their experience.

For example, the Bible truth, "God is a good God" can be the basis for an endless variety of guided conversations in the various Bible Learning Activities. While participating in a nature activity, as children experience with their senses some aspect of His creation, you can repeat the truth, "God is a good God" in different ways so they can appreciate God's goodness in creating the world and all that is in it. During an art activity, you can sing, "Suzie's fingers paint, paint, paint," then ask, "Who made Suzie's fingers?" After Suzie says, "God did," then you say, "God is a good God!" Then move on and sing, "Billy's fingers paint, paint, paint."

Preschoolers Learn Through Their Senses

The second characteristic of the young child you should always keep in mind is this: THEY LEARN THROUGH THEIR SENSES on a concrete level. BLAs are sensory experiences, that is, they involve the young child's senses of sight, smell, touch, taste, and hearing. As they encounter the world of their classroom, you continually guide them to think about that world in terms of the Biblical truth for that particular session. Remember, that's as they encounter it. You are there experiencing it with them, guiding their conversation toward God.

Examples of Bible Learning Activities for each of the seven categories listed above can be found in the Appendix. But, before you turn to those examples, let us share one further thought about selecting them: don't worry about having to think up new ideas each week. The curriculum your church provides will give you specifics on which BLA to use each week, what specific materials you'll need, and suggestions for your guided conversation. Trust your curriculum. You don't teach it; you teach the Bible. But your curriculum will give you tremendous help in doing your best each week.

In each of the seven BLAs for this age group, your role will be the same even though the specifics will change. You should:

• Supervise the play at all times to ensure the safety of the children as well as the healthy involvement of all the learners, even the shy ones.

• Suggest ideas for play to stimulate the children's involvement and to direct their play in order to provide natural opportunities for talking about the Bible truth for the day.

• Guide the conversation through song and word in such a way that the Bible truth is woven through their sensory experiences.

• Plan ways to use books and pictures to reinforce the Bible theme.

Remember, you are the guide for a group of active learners, not the performer for a group of passive listeners.

BLAs for Children, Youth, and Adults

The basic operating principle behind Bible Learning Activities is a process called synthesis. The easiest way to understand synthesis is to think of baking a cake. In any BLA, ingredients are brought in, sifted, stirred into what is already known, spices added, placed in the oven, and the end result is a learning "cake." That's synthesis—the process of bringing in new information, attitudes, and experiences and shaping them into something else that helps us learn.

As you use BLAs, remember that the least important aspect of the process is what the cake looks like when it comes out of the oven. The active handling of the ingredients (God's Word) with a well-defined goal is what really matters.

Your challenge in using BLAs is to select methods which have three characteristics:

1. they must support your learning objectives;
2. they must be appropriate for your own unique class, with consideration given to the age, maturity level, and individual interests of your "sheep;"
3. they must provide for meaningful involvement.

BLAs for children, youth, and adults can be grouped into six general categories. The difference is in the focus and the difficulty of the individual activities. The six categories are:

- Verbal activities
- Writing activities
- Art
- Music
- Drama
- Miscellaneous

Children's Division

If you are a teacher of those wonderful, carefree, rambunctious children in the elementary grades (first grade through fifth or sixth grade), yours is a special challenge and a special treat. Research shows that in our generation more people come into a relationship with Jesus during these years of childhood than at any other age.

Bible Learning Activities are effective tools for involving children in the study of the Bible during this impressionable time. They provide a wide diversity of interesting experiences that lend themselves to encouraging the practical application of Biblical truth to everyday life.

Fortunately, your curriculum will provide a steady stream of ideas for BLAs that are lesson-related. You don't have to worry about making them up Sunday after Sunday. If, however, you would like to know more about the BLAs that are appropriate for this age group a list of examples for each of the six categories can be found in the Appendix. You will also find additional help in the resources listed below.

Bible Alive: Creative Projects for Bible Learning by Lin Johnson (Standard #14-03073)

Learning Games and Activities for All Ages by Elizabeth Whitney Crisci (Standard #14-03080)

Let the Games Begin: Creative Games for Teaching Scripture by Bev Gundersen (Standard #14-03081)

Bulletin Board Activity Centers by Judy Dorsett (Standard #14-03284)

Fun Ideas for Bible Memory by Barbara Lockwood (Standard #14-03075)

How To Do Bible Learning Activities (Grades 1-6) by Barbara Bolton (International Center for Learning)

Youth Division

If you are a teacher of teens, you have a special challenge. Your students are unpredictable beings who lurk in the forests of adolescence, hovering between childhood and adulthood. And though you may not feel it or hear it from their lips, these special people need you and love you.

While it is true that more elementary school children come to Christ than people from any other age group, the depth of commitment that leads to life-long devotion to Jesus is most often nurtured during the exuberant years of adolescence.

Bible Learning Activities are effective tools for involving youth in the study of the Bible during these years of growing toward adult life. BLAs provide a wide diversity of interesting experiences that lend themselves to encouraging the practical application of Bible truth to everyday life.

The list found in the Appendix will provide you with an introduction to creative Bible Learning Activities for Youth. There are many other good resources to help you as well, but their effectiveness depends on your willingness to use them. Remember, your class time is filled with activity. Will it be your activity, or will it be you directing their activity and the increased learning that ensues? See the following resources for additional help.

Message in Motion: Simulation Games for Teens by Tim Jones (Standard #14-03060)

Teens Can Make a Difference: Helping Them Take a Stand by Kathleen M. Zaffore (Standard #14-03233)

Creative Bible Studies (Volumes 1 and 2) by Dennis Benson (Group Books)

Youth Ministry Cargo (Group Books)

Ideas (Volumes 1-38) by Youth Specialities

Adult Division

One renowned educator has said, "Jesus taught adults and played with children. Maybe some of us need to face up to the fact that we are doing just the opposite!"

The Bible is an adult book, written by adults for adults, on adult themes, by a God who requires that adults take up their crosses and follow Him. Of all age levels, the effect of regular study of God's Word should be seen in practical, sacrificial ministry response among adults more than any other.

Adults are capable of responding seriously to the truth of God's Word, but too often Sunday-school classes provide comfortable places to be "blessed" and "to grow," rather than places to be nurtured, challenged, trained, and organized for ministry in the world. You may find the list found in the Appendix helpful in using Bible Learning Activities with adults. For additional help, see the following resources.

You Can Teach Adults Successfully (Standard #14-03208)

Strengthening the Adult Sunday School Class by Dick Murray (Abingdon)

Group Talk! by Ed Stewart and Nina Fishwick (Regal)

Now let's rejoin the training/planning meeting.

8

"If you aim at nothing, you'll hit it every time."
— Anonymous

Planning Makes the Doing Productive

"Thank you for showing that filmstrip on Bible Learning Activities, Diane. It stretched my thinking about what actually goes on in a Sunday-school class and gave me tons of new ideas. I'm looking forward to putting them to work this Sunday." Joe beamed a smile of appreciation to Diane, then sipped his coffee, hoping she would carry on the conversation. He had cornered her at the beginning of their ten-minute break.

Plan Training Sessions To Meet Individual Needs

"I'm glad you liked it. Betty Spate suggested I focus this month's training session on BLAs. She said you and Sally would appreciate it."

"I should have known," Joe said. "She is something else!"

Sally just smiled.

"Yes, she's a good friend, so I'm happy to accommodate her simple request," Diane responded.

Sally's smile remained on her face as she framed her own words of thanks. "I appreciate the training session, too, Diane, as well as the warm reception you and the other teachers have given me. I'm looking forward to taking my place on Sunday morning."

Diane was pleased to have two such sincere and willing people working with her. "We're delighted that you both are with us. You've started out the right way by getting involved in our training/planning meetings."

"I didn't start out so right," Joe said. "I wouldn't be here tonight if Betty hadn't stopped me in the hall one Sunday to ask how things were going in the class. That led to two long discussions. One even included the pastor. The fact of the matter is, I was so frustrated that I had considered quitting."

How Not To Recruit and Train

"I knew you were having difficulty," Diane said. "It's partly my fault."

"Your fault?" Joe said with surprise in his voice.

"Yes, my fault. We have always worked as a department, different groups functioning together in the same room. We plan together and work together on Sunday mornings to guide the children through a variety of large and small group activities. When you were recruited, we needed someone in a hurry. We didn't give you time to observe the department in action, like Sally's doing. We didn't sit down with you and give you a clear explanation of how we do things. And we didn't make enough effort to involve you in these meetings."

"You mean I'm supposed to be in the room with the rest of you?" Joe was incredulous.

"Yes." Diane said with embarrassment in her voice.

"Now I understand. That first Sunday, I was almost angry with the rest of you for making so much noise while I was trying to talk. That's why I asked if it was all right to move my boys into the little room down the hall."

"I'm sorry, Joe," Diane said. "We just thought you understood how we operated. That first Sunday was a surprise to us, too. When you didn't participate with the department, we weren't sure what to think. We all were concerned and hoped that the problem would work itself out. But by itself, it never would."

"But the Lord has worked it out for us!" Sally said, still radiating that big smile. "And if it had happened another way, I probably wouldn't be here wanting to help. My interest was stirred during the talks with Betty and Dave. For the first time, I saw what God could do through me, and I wanted Him to do it."

"Then let's quit apologizing and get back to business." Joe's happy remark was perfectly timed. It was the end of the break.

Noticing some teachers going to another room, Joe asked, "Why are they leaving?"

"Because we're making too much noise," Sally injected. Joe picked up on his wife's barb immediately and laughed deeply, washing away some of the self-consciousness that he still was feeling.

Tailor the Learning Experience To Each Age Level

"That may be part of it, Sally, but the main reason is that after our block of training, and when it's time to plan out sessions, we work only with the team that functions together on Sunday morning." The questioning look on Sally's face encouraged Diane to continue. "You see, even though our curriculum materials are similar, and even though our class time is structured the same, we have to tailor the learning experiences to Juniors. They are different from Primary and Middler children in many ways, so both need their own specially planned class times."

"I remember discussing differences in learners with Betty and Dave," Sally said.

"So after we train together on subjects common to children's teachers, we split off into our respective departments and plan our lessons for a whole month."

"A whole month!" Joe was amazed. He had never thought of planning a month at a time, let alone planning and working with the others. It was so simple, yet so obviously right. "That beats my Saturday night planning hands down."

Planning Is Important

"It surely does," Diane continued. "We firmly believe that PLANNING MAKES THE DOING PRODUCTIVE. So the better we plan and prepare, the more effective our class time. Together we pray for our kids, talk about their special needs and anything unusual that happened in the last month that might influence our teaching in the coming month. Then we discuss the unit aims and select the learning objectives for each individual lesson."

"That's what determines which BLA you use, right?" Sally was getting more interested all the time.

"Right!" Diane said. "We make sure we all clearly comprehend those objectives. Because we work as a team, we have to be sure that we all are headed in the same direction.

"Once we have thought about our learners and set our objectives, then we begin to plan the individual sessions. We discuss which methods will work the best with our learners and the specific objectives. We make sure we identify a key word/theme for each lesson. We then decide what materials to use in order for learning to occur. We pray once more that God would use our efforts and our class time to draw people closer to Him."

"That sounds like a lot of work," Joe said, with a trace of the what-have-I-got-myself-into attitude showing through.

Planning Saves Time

"It is work. But we volunteered to work. And I'll promise you one thing: One to one-and-a-half hours per month planning as a group means a whole lot less time wasted as individuals." Diane's complete confidence in the value of planning together was showing through. "But even more important than that, when we put our best efforts into planning and preparing, God is honored, and our learners have a far better learning experience. It is worth every minute!"

"I'm convinced, I'm convinced," Joe said, as he raised his hands and feigned resignation. "I just wish it were this clearcut in the adult area."

"Oh, it is!" Diane responded. "The only difference is in the way the hour is structured. Leadership teams of adult classes should be planning and training together, too. For that matter, teachers in all age levels should be working together."

Team-up In Age-level Groups

Reader: Diane's comment is true. Even in a very small church, it is possible to build a team of people who work together in the teaching ministry. Several heads and hearts are better than one.

The key is to work together in age-level groups. In that way, you have the advantage of teaming up with other teachers who deal with learners with similar characteristics. You will share learning objectives, Bible Learning Activities, and the hour of precious time you have with your learners.

To plan more effectively, you should be aware of the best way to organize your class time for the age level you teach. Follow the instructions below to explore the specifics for your class:

- If you teach preschoolers, keep reading below;
- If you teach elementary-age children turn to page 75;
- If you teach teens (grades 5/6—12) turn to page 76;
- If you teach adults (age 18 and up), turn to page 78;
- If you are interested in all ages groups—keep reading.

Early Childhood Division

Because your learners are in the early stages of development, your class time will have a very different structure than that of the other age levels. It is built around three basic parts:

- Bible Learning Centers
- Group Time
- Bible Story/Activity Page

The first part is where you use the Bible Learning Activities we discussed in the previous chapter. Each Sunday, you will select a variety of BLAs and organize your room into BIBLE LEARNING CENTERS in which these activities take place. The number of different centers depends on the size of your class and the number of teachers working in the department. A rule of thumb is one center for every five children with a teacher supervising each and guiding the conversation to the Bible truth for the day.

Bible Learning Centers are first in the schedule for several reasons. You want learning to begin as the children walk through the door. As the department leader warmly meets the child at the door, she prepares him/her for a good morning. Coats and belongings are cared for, then the child is directed to choose one of the different BLAs. Immediately, that child is met by the teacher in charge of the center the child chooses and the meaningful activity begins!

Teach Children the Way God Made Them

Also, children do not come into the room ready to sit down and listen. God built them with wiggles and squirms and energy. By allowing the children to choose the center in which they want to work, their interest is captured and they are more likely to be engaged in constructive play than in destructive, negative behavior. Cooperating with the development of the child solves a multitude of discipline challenges and makes the teaching/learning process come alive.

During Bible Learning Centers' time, children are allowed to move freely between centers. When their interest fades in one, they simply move to another (as long as there is room at the new center). That is perfectly all right. All the centers are thematic in nature, focused on the lesson theme, and that theme will be reinforced in whichever center the child chooses.

This allows for a broad diversity of interests and attention spans while maximizing the ability of teachers to guide conversation to the Bible truth.

"But," you ask, "when does the playing end and the learning begin?"

Answer: They are one and the same! The young child learns through play, as much or more than s/he learns through instruction. Remember, these are not miniature adults.

Bible Learning Activities conclude when the department leader sings or plays a song quietly on the tape player. This is the signal for teachers to guide learners in putting blocks, puzzles, or books away, straightening the Family Living Center, or cleaning up the Nature Center.

As children finish their housekeeping chores, they gather in a circle at the GROUP TIME rug where the department leader is already involving the early arrivers. She greets the gathering children with songs like: "I have a friend on Sunday morning, is her name." Or she asks questions like: "Tell us, , what did you do with the pine cones this morning?"

Group Time allows for activities that would be distracting if they were done in the Bible Learning Centers. All the teachers in the department should participate in the circle or the Group Time. Group songs, complete with marching or motions, finger fun, use of tape recorders or phonographs, conversations, and prayer time all provide a positive change of pace, as well as further opportunities to focus little ones' attention on the session topic.

Activities Build Relationships

Also, the department leader has an opportunity to build a sense of group identity. By sitting, singing, listening, marching, and praying together, a relationship is developed. It is important for all adults to be involved with the children in the Group Time. Just be aware that not all children will be comfortable in the group. Some will be eager beavers, others will want to stand just outside the circle and watch, still others will have no apparent interest in the group. Don't let the differences in response upset you. It's okay for a child to keep his distance. That doesn't mean he's not participating. However, it is our experience that when teachers provide meaningful activities, the child will generally be drawn to them.

Finally, the BIBLE STORY/ACTIVITY PAGE wraps up the hour. In small, permanently-assigned groups of four to six, teachers share the Bible story from which the Bible truth is taken. Remember though, with young children your aim is not for them to remember every fact of the story. It is for them to hear and comprehend what is at the heart of the story in a way that influences their everyday living.

After the many times the Bible truth is repeated during the Bible Learning Activities, hearing it again in the Bible story is a reinforcement, not the introduction of a new idea. Then, when they get to think about it one more time as they complete their Activity Pages, a further reinforcement takes place.

"What part of my hour should each of these segments occupy?" you may ask.

Good question. The answer is different for 2's and 3's than it is for 4's and 5's. Basically, the Bible Learning Centers occupy one half to three quarters of the session, with the other two segments sharing the remaining time.

A Suggested Schedule for Preschoolers

SUNDAY SCHOOL SESSION
2's and 3's

BIBLE LEARNING CENTERS	40–45 minutes
GROUP TIME	10–15 minutes
BIBLE STORY/ACTIVITY PAGE	10–15 minutes

SUNDAY SCHOOL SESSION
4's and 5's

BIBLE LEARNING CENTERS	35–40 minutes
GROUP TIME	10–15 minutes
BIBLE STORY/ACTIVITY PAGE	15–20 minutes

Both schedules include time for transitioning between segments of the session.

There it is! Your basic introduction to the best way to structure the Sunday school hour for the Early Childhood Division. Be sure to check the introductory pages of your teacher's manual for more help in structuring your own class time this way.

Now turn to page 79 to rejoin Joe, Sally, and Diane as they conclude their planning meeting.

Children's Division

You want to structure the time with your children in a way that cooperates with their developmental stage. The first step is to create interest. Next, you steer their interest to the Bible. Then, you guide them to consider what God wants them to learn from the Bible. Finally, they are allowed to express what they have learned in different ways that help them own the truth.

The parts of your session should correspond to these four steps. As children enter the room, they are greeted by the department leader and directed to their permanent class group which is already engaged in BIBLE READINESS ACTIVITIES (step one). During this time children participate in research projects, work on memory verses, prepare an item for the Bible story, etc. It is an active time designed to capture their interest, immediately engage them in activity, and prepare them with background information for the Bible lesson.

Next comes BIBLE EXPLORATION (step two). Again, this takes place in the permanent class groups. During this segment, the teacher presents the Bible story in any of a number of ways: telling it, visualizing it with flannelgraph figures or puppets, acting it out, showing it on a video cassette, etc. You should consciously draw out children's insights, allowing them to express what they have discovered in the first part of the session about the story or its background.

The third part of the session is BIBLE APPLICATION (steps three and four). Children are guided to explore ways the Bible truth relates to their own lives. Then they make a decision to respond to God's Word in practical ways throughout the week.

As we close the session, children leave their permanent class groups and gather as a department for Bible sharing, singing, learning games, and further reinforcement of how the Bible truth for the day relates to their lives.

In a sixty-minute session, you should spend twenty to twenty-five minutes allowing the children to engage fully in the BIBLE READINESS ACTIVITIES. Primaries should be given the longer time here because their attention spans are shorter. The action and variety of the activities keep their interest high. Even with Juniors, though, twenty minutes is minimum.

The remaining time should be divided between BIBLE EXPLORATION, BIBLE APPLICATION, and CLOSE THE SESSION.

Suggested Schedule for Children

SUNDAY SCHOOL SESSION
Elementary Children

BIBLE READINESS ACTIVITIES	20-25 minutes
BIBLE EXPLORATION	15 minutes
BIBLE APPLICATION	10-20 minutes
CLOSE THE SESSION	10-15 minutes

There it is—a basic introduction to the best way to structure the Sunday school hour for the Children's Division. Be sure to check the introductory pages in your teacher's manual for more help in structuring your own class time this way.

Now turn to page 79 to rejoin Joe, Sally, and Diane as they conclude their planning meeting.

Youth Division

You want to structure the time with your teens in a way that cooperates with their developmental stage. The first step is to create interest. Next, you steer their interest to the Bible. Then, you guide them to consider what God wants them to learn from the Bible. Finally, they are encouraged to express what they have learned in different ways that help them own the truth.

The parts of your session correspond to these four steps. As teens enter the room, you should get their ATTENTION (step one). We learn nothing until we are focused on the object of our study. And for most teens, studying is the last thing they really want to do on Sunday morning. This is an active time designed to capture their interest, immediately engage them in activity, and prepare them with background information for the Bible lesson.

Your curriculum will give you plenty of help in planning for this time. But the responsibility of setting the learning environment is yours. You choose whether to engage them in a lesson-related activity as they walk through the door or to let them use ten minutes talking about the ball game or the party while they wait for class "to begin."

The next section is INTO THE WORD (step two). Once the learners' interest is focused on the session topic, then your job is to help them explore and discover what God's Word has to say about that topic. The more active they are in this process, the better. Use Bible Learning Activities to the best advantage here. Don't try to hold eight seventh-grade boys in rapt attention for twenty-five minutes.

The next part of your session is INTO LIFE (step three). It is the time in which you guide your teens to discuss what God's truth means in relation to their world and their lives.

The final part of the session is COMMITMENT (step four). Learners are challenged to let God do His work in their lives in this one particular area.

How much time will you give to each of these session parts? That depends on the lesson you are planning. If it is a very familiar passage, you probably will minimize INTO THE WORD and maximize INTO LIFE. That way, more time is spent exploring life applications of a familiar passage than reviewing familiar material.

On the other hand, if the Bible passage is unfamiliar, or very difficult, or contains a message the teens might miss, you want to give INTO THE WORD as much time as needed. When adequate time is spent in Bible exploration and discovery, meaningful life application will occur.

A Suggested Schedule for Teens

SUNDAY SCHOOL SESSION
Youth

ATTENTION	10 minutes
INTO THE WORD	25-30 minutes
INTO LIFE	15-20 minutes
COMMITMENT	10-15 minutes

There it is—a basic introduction to the best way to structure the Sunday school hour for the Youth Division. Be sure to check the introductory pages of your teacher's manual for more help in structuring your own class time this way.

Now turn to page 79 to rejoin Joe, Sally, and Diane as they conclude their planning meeting.

Adult Division

As a teacher of adults, you want to structure your class time in a way that maximizes the learning that takes place. The first step is to create interest. Next, you steer their interest to the Bible. Then, you guide them to consider what God wants them to learn from the Bible. Finally, they are encouraged to express what they have learned in different ways that help them own the truth.

The parts of your session correspond to these four steps. Your first task is to get their attention. Nothing is learned until we are focused on the object of our study. You must get them INTO THE LESSON (step one) by involving them in activity which focuses their interest on the session topic or theme.

Your curriculum will give you plenty of help in planning for this time. By the way, please use printed curriculum. Studies show that more than fifty percent of adult teachers use no curriculum resources. They often boast about "teaching the Bible, not curriculum."

That is an unfortunate misunderstanding. People never study curriculum. Curriculum is the tool to help you teach the Bible in varied, interesting, and meaningful ways week after week, year after year. It is developed by professionals to support you as you lead your adults into the Bible.

The responsibility of setting the learning environment is yours. You choose whether to engage them in a lesson-related activity as they walk through the door or to let them use ten minutes talking about the ball game or the weather while they wait for class "to begin."

The next section is INTO THE WORD (step two). Once learners' interest is focused on the session topic, then your job is to help them explore and discover what God's Word has to say about that topic. The more active they are in this process, the better. Use Bible Learning Activities to the best advantage here.

Lecture is the most commonly used Bible Learning Activity, but it is by no means the only one. It's a good one, but don't overuse it. Remember, PEOPLE LEARN BEST WHEN THEY ARE INVOLVED. Vary your approach, and when you do lecture, make sure you lecture with enthusiasm, and do all you can to involve your learners with visuals and handouts.

The final part of your session combines steps three and four. INTO LIFE is the time in which you guide your learners to discuss what God's truth means in relation to their world and their lives. They are challenged to let God do His work in their lives in this one particular area.

How much time will you give to each of these session parts? That depends on the lesson you are planning. If it is a very familiar passage, then you probably will minimize INTO THE WORD and maximize INTO LIFE. That way, more time is spent exploring life applications of a familiar passage than reviewing familiar material.

On the other hand, if the Bible passage is unfamiliar, or very difficult, or contains a message the learners might miss, you will want to give INTO THE WORD as much time as needed. When adequate time is spent in Bible exploration and discovery, meaningful life application will occur.

A Suggested Schedule for Adults

SUNDAY SCHOOL SESSION
Adults

INTO THE LESSON	10-15 minutes
INTO THE WORD	25-30 minutes
INTO LIFE	25-30 minutes

There it is—a basic introduction to the best way to structure the Sunday school hour for the Adult Division. Be sure to check the introductory pages in your teacher's manual for more help in structuring your own class time this way.

Now let's rejoin Joe, Sally, and Diane as they conclude their planning meeting.

"I can hardly believe it," Joe said to Sally in the car on the way home from the meeting. "In two short hours I learned about Bible Learning Activities, working together as a department, the best way to use my hour, and I have begun preparation for a whole month's worth of lessons."

"I'm excited, too," Sally exclaimed, as she squeezed his arm. "A month ago, teaching children was the furthest thing from my mind. Now, I can hardly wait to get started."

"I've thought a lot about this since that morning Betty stopped me in the hall. How could I have been so ignorant? I've been in Sunday school all my life and had no clue that there was such a wide, wonderful aspect to it," Joe responded.

Sally nodded her agreement as Joe continued, "It makes me wonder where our priorities are. I had to spend years in college to get my engineering degree, and I still had to go through a difficult exam to get my license. I think that's the way it should be, because our mistakes mean people's lives are in danger.

"But it seems odd to me," Joe continued, "that when the eternal destiny of people is involved, even their success in living for God while they're on earth . . . " He paused, and spoke thoughtfully, "It seems odd to me that we put a teacher's manual and a Bible into the responsible person's hand, pat him on the back, and say, 'If you need help, see me.'"

Teaching God's Word Deserves Our Best Effort

"I know what you mean," Sally responded. "I'm glad our church has training/planning meetings. I know they'll make a difference. But you almost slipped through the cracks and never understood . . ."

"Never understood anything," he interrupted, "until someone who cared took time with me. Sally, let's remember that. And when we are the veterans, let's make new teachers our personal responsibility, especially taking them under our wings like Betty has done with us."

Sally smiled at Joe. During the rest of the ride home they quietly enjoyed the feeling of purpose that was beginning to spring up in both their hearts.

9

"A wise teacher makes learning a joy."
— Proverbs 15:2

A Checklist for Review

At the end of this chapter we have placed the image of a clipboard. On this clipboard we've listed the basic concepts of teaching described in this book.

This little clipboard is intended to help you remember these concepts. We want you to use them as a yardstick to measure yourself. We want them to be a constant reminder of what you are doing and why you are doing it.

Basic Concepts for Teaching the Bible

So before you finish reading this book, let's take one more look at these basic concepts.

TEACHERS ARE MADE, NOT BORN. Has that become an ownable concept yet? You can become a truly effective teacher, helping people discover and explore the new life in Christ. To develop into an effective teacher, you must be willing to invest some ongoing time and energy. Growth as a teacher depends on your investment of time and energy.

The process begins as you KNOW THYSELF. Keep in mind

your own learning preferences as you design learning experiences for others. In doing that, you will be reminded that they may have different learning preferences. Be honest about your motivations with yourself and God. Why are you doing what you are doing? What do you want to accomplish? What is your commitment level?

TEACHERS TEACH PEOPLE, NOT INFORMATION. That means as you are planning and implementing your class sessions, your "sheep" have to be uppermost in your mind. Get to know them, both as individuals and as a group, as people with their own unique personalities, and as people passing through well-defined developmental stages.

Why do we teach these unique individuals for whom Jesus died? Our goal is REACHING AND TEACHING PEOPLE TO KNOW GOD. We want them to come into a relationship with Jesus Christ and to grow in that relationship by becoming more like Him in their thinking, feeling, and doing.

God has given His Word to help in that task, so THE CONTENT OF OUR TEACHING IS THE BIBLE. It is alive and powerful because God reveals Himself in it. As we study the Bible, we often meet ourselves because we are so like the characters in the stories. We discover that it is as applicable today as the day it was written.

In order to have the maximum impact on the lives of our "sheep," we have to cooperate with the way God designed people for learning: PEOPLE LEARN BEST WHEN THEY ARE INVOLVED. There should always be activity in our classrooms. The question is whether the activity is teacher-centered or learner-centered. The learning process should include Bible Learning Activities which provide a broad variety of involvement methods. Use them wisely.

In conclusion, we reap what we sow. GROWING NEVER STOPS, TRAINING NEVER ENDS. We must work together to strengthen and equip each other to meet our mutual goals. And as a team, PLANNING MAKES THE DOING PRODUCTIVE. If several workers train and plan together, using time in the best possible way, then the harvest is certain to be greater.

May God richly bless you as you grow in the privileged, joyous, sometimes frustrating, always rewarding calling that we call TEACHING!

Note: We encourage you to use the clipboard summary on the next page as a resource for training others in your Sunday school. Feel free to copy it or use it as an overhead transparency master (for classroom use only).

Teacher's Personal Growth Checklist

____ 1. Teachers Are Made, Not Born
—I want to grow as a teacher.

____ 2. Know Thyself
—I know my own motivation and learning-style preference.

____ 3. Teachers Teach People, Not Information
—I know my "sheep" and I know their age-level characteristics.

____ 4. Reaching and Teaching People to Know God
—My efforts are focused on building people in their relationship to Jesus.

____ 5. The Content of Our Teaching Is the Bible
—I understand the way I approach teaching the Bible and try to build on that strength.

____ 6. People Learn Best When They Are Involved
—I work hard to make sure that, by using Bible Learning Activities, my learners are as involved as I am.

____ 7. Planning Makes the Doing Productive
—I work with others in my age-level to plan and implement lessons.

Appendix

Bible Learning Activities

Bible Learning Activities for the Early Childhood Division

1. FAMILY LIVING: In a pretend setting like his own home, the young child relives life in a family over and over. The Biblical concepts of sharing, loving, helping, caring, and others are naturally practiced in the spontaneous play of the Family Living Center.

A good teacher not only guides the conversation that takes place in this BLA toward the Bible truth, s/he also can gain insight into the individual children, their feelings, interests, fears, and self-concept. That helps as we teach people, not information.

MATERIALS: There should be child-size (not Barbie doll-size) furnishings for kitchen play and for doll care. Doll bed, blankets, a simple doll, wooden sink, stove, and refrigerator; unbreakable dishes, empty food boxes, small broom, etc. Rule of thumb: Don't include anything small enough to be put into little mouths.

2. BLOCKS: Playing with blocks is a joy of childhood. These many-sized playthings are favorites because they are so versatile. They provide large muscle activity, they allow for the exercise of the imagination, and they are great for one child working alone or for several children playing together.

Because of this versatility, the Block Center is a wonderful tool in the hands of the young child's teacher. The socializing that occurs during the play provides ample opportunity to guide the conversation toward the Bible truth on which your class is focusing that day.

Expect the 2's to hold a block or carry it around without being too interested in constructing anything. The 5-year-olds, on the other side of the spectrum, will aggressively build structures ranging from the house in the Bible story last week to a fire truck. Remember that for all ages, the play in which they are engaged is more important than whatever structures they build. Use the play as opportunity for teaching.

MATERIALS: 2's and 3's need large, lightweight hollow cardboard blocks, even blocks made from milk cartons or other similar containers. 3's enjoy more variety, so include different sizes and shapes, but still lightweight. 4's & 5's build more ambitious projects, so they need many more blocks with a wide variety of shapes and sizes and colors. The sets of wooden blocks for institutional use are the best investment. They are large with a clear, durable finish unlike the toy varieties found in department stores.

Wooden or plastic animals, people, and transportation toys may also enhance the theme. To add even more variety, use poster board or butcher paper as backdrops for play in the Block Center. Draw an appropriate landscape or building scene on the paper, then tape it to the wall behind the blocks or place it on the floor under the blocks. You will be surprised how well the children will respond to the scenery.

3. NATURE: There is no other Bible Learning Activity for young children that allows so much freedom for their curiosity as nature activities. Seeing, feeling, smelling, tasting, even listening to the things God has created is a joy for children—and the variety is endless! From tasting fresh picked grain in autumn to feeling the furry warmth of an animal, God's creation is a source of joy and amazement.

The variety of experiences possible with this BLA also makes it a favorite with teachers. Bible truths ranging from "God made all things" to "Be kind to one another" are reinforced naturally in the interaction that occurs at this center.

MATERIALS: The list is so long, we will just mention a few ideas. Your curriculum will give you appropriate lesson-related suggestions.

- Planting seeds
- Tasting different fruits or vegetables
- Handling magnets
- Taking nature walk
- A sand table
- Water play
- Manipulating a variety of materials
- Viewing and touching animals

4. BOOKS: These faithful friends are an important part of the learning environment for young children. They allow children to relive familiar experiences, remind them of objects and events, and encourage them to have new experiences without leaving the security of your classroom.

Christian teachers concerned with laying a good foundation for knowing God often feel that the only books used in the Sunday school should be Bible story books. While these certainly are appropriate, other books which relate to the lesson theme are important also. Remember, the teacher of the young child is as concerned with repeating a single concept in as many ways as possible and relating it to their limited worlds, as they are with having a three-year-old remember a Bible story.

That leads back to a basic principle that is true of every BLA: You should select activities and materials for one purpose and one purpose only—to help you meet the learning objectives you have for that particular lesson. To maximize the effectiveness of your few minutes with these children, everything should relate to the lesson theme.

MATERIALS: For 2's and 3's, picture books are ideal. Large and colorful illustrations of familiar objects or situations are the best. 4's and 5's will enjoy picture books with text of varying levels of difficultly. Try to provide a good selection. Of course, they need to be lesson related.

The best source from which to choose the books your church should purchase is your curriculum. The books suggested in it are carefully chosen because of their relation to the lesson aims. Many times, these books are available in your church library, the children's section of your local library, Christian book stores, or even at garage sales.

The most important book that you use is the Bible. Young children should see it in your classroom. They should see you use it as you tell them stories from it. They should sense your love and appreciation for it. At this stage of their young lives, the impressions they receive about God, the Bible, and the church are as important as specific knowledge they might acquire about those three. One technique that some teachers have adopted to help make their use of the Bible more apparent is to paperclip the pictures from their teaching resource material to pages in their Bible, then hold it up to show the pictures.

5. PUZZLES: Puzzles often are associated with the book area and are in a real sense companions to books. The large pictures that are used, the left-right eye coordination exercised, and the familiar scenes and objects that are subjects of the puzzles all form a close bond with books.

MATERIALS: Puzzles for the Early Childhood Division should be chosen to match the abilities of the age-level involved. The best kind are the wooden inlay-type jigsaw puzzles in which the border of the puzzle forms a natural tray-like rim around the actual pieces. Two-year-olds should have simple puzzles with whole pictures intact and a maximum of four or five separate pieces, such as a puzzle with four different animals on it, each image occupying one whole puzzle piece. Small wooden handles protruding from the surface help the little ones manipulate the pieces. The complexity of the puzzles should increase to include puzzles of as many as ten to twenty pieces for five year olds.

Invest in good, wooden puzzles and a good puzzle rack, but supplement them with your originals. Make puzzles by gluing a teaching picture on masonite. Then cut it out with a jig saw. Or make shapes out of felt and allow children to create their own pictures on a felt-covered board.

6. MUSIC: Of all the Bible Learning Activities used with the young child, none intimidates teachers as much as music. But no other activity has the same powerful impact on children as music does. Unfortunately, adults often perceive themselves as having no musical ability, thus they shy away from using music more than absolutely necessary.

But that is the adult's problem. Children have no such prejudice. Watch them. In uninterrupted play, they will be active for only a very short time before they begin singing or humming or chanting, even if it is complete nonsense. This is a beautifully natural form of expression that God has given and they are completely oblivious to your concerns. An adult with a fabulous voice or a tin-eared monotone are both the same to them.

So use music as a Bible Learning Activity by itself, as well as using it throughout your entire session. Use it naturally and spontaneously, just like they do. Forget the idea of a "song service." Integrate music into the whole experience.

From time to time include simple rhythm instruments. Children will sometimes make up their own songs related to the lesson theme. Encourage them to be creative. Look to your curriculum for lots of good music ideas.

7. ART: Activities using crayons, paints, clay, paper, etc. are the most familiar of all learning activities, especially to proud parents whose refrigerator doors are covered with Sunday morning masterpieces. But art activities are often misunderstood or misused by teachers.

The key to the effective use of art activities in Bible learning is the same simple principle that underlies all BLAs—the teaching value is in the process, not the product. We are not trying to create young artists. We are trying to create learning experiences in which teachable moments occur in the interaction between teacher and child. This kind of experience or activity makes lasting impressions about God.

Use art materials often. Supervise carefully but participate fully. Affirm the children as they express themselves and take every opportunity to guide the conversation to the Bible truth for the day. "Johnny's sun is so yellow. I'm thankful that God made the sun."

MATERIALS: Again, your curriculum will give you a constant stream of good ideas for art activities, but here are a few suggestions:

- Painting with hands, brushes, sponges or other implements;
- Using clay or dough activities that provide pleasurable touch;
- Drawing with crayons, or coloring pictures;
- Cutting paper and pasting or taping it together.

Bible Learning Activities for the Children's Division

1. VERBAL ACTIVITIES: Children love to talk! Expressing oneself is as important to the learning process as bringing in new ideas. In fact, it is the other side of the same coin. New ideas and information become my ideas and information only when they are processed and accepted. In order to express himself in a way that is satisfying, a child must first have good input and then process it so that it can be expressed. Thus, expression and ownership go hand in hand.

The variety of Verbal Activities is very wide. Consider a few:

- STORYTELLING: Of course this includes you telling the children Bible stories or telling them stories that illustrate the Bible truth. This is a favorite, especially in the lower grades. But don't forget that children love to tell stories, too. When you combine the storytelling with art activities in which they create visuals to go along with their stories, you have a great formula for learning.
- DISCUSSION: This is not like a true adult discussion in which learners exchange ideas. This is more like "question and answer." Groups of six or seven children seated in a circle respond to your carefully worded questions. Your questions

are meant to stimulate their thinking about what God was doing with the people in a Bible story and what God is doing in their hearts. Most children in elementary school enjoy talking about their thoughts and feelings. Remember to lead the talking times in ways appropriate to the age of the talkers.

• BRAINSTORMING: This is simply saying, "Let's list as many different ______ as we can in two minutes." They love it and you'll be surprised at their resourcefulness!

2. WRITING ACTIVITIES: Yes, this includes filling in the spaces in the handouts you distribute in class. But stretch your horizons! Writing is a great way to help children think about the Bible truth you are studying. The old adage among writers is, "You can't write it if you don't understand it." Writing your thoughts requires more mental effort than simply speaking them because it requires more understanding of the subject of your thoughts.

Writing activities are great, but remember that it's the making of the cake that is important, not the cake itself. You are not a school teacher charged with correcting spelling errors and improving handwriting. You are charged with reaching and teaching people to know God.

Consider using a few of these writing activities:

• JOURNAL: In a study of a character's life that stretches over several weeks, or that lasts only one week, ask children to write a "Dear Diary" entry from the main character's point of view. Or assign each child a different character from the story. Or create a situation in life today in which a person experiences something similar to the Bible character, then let the learners write from that person's perspective.

• NEWSPAPER: Work together to publish a JERUSALEM TIMES or a BETHLEHEM HERALD or the like. Different children write the various sections of a paper.

• POETRY: There is traditional verse (they write it all or you provide one verse, they provide the next, as individuals or as a group). There is also free verse and haiku which is three lines with a specific number of syllables in each line (five, seven, and, five, unrhymed).

IMPORTANT: When using writing activities, you need to be aware of the wide differences in the ability and interest levels of your children. It's OK if Suzie chooses not to write. There's a reason. Involve her as your helper, distributing materials, etc.

3. ART: This is a perennial favorite of children's teachers! Because this category is limited only by your own imagination, we'll simply lay out a few concepts and list a variety of art media. You do the rest. Your curriculum will give you lots of help, too.

Art activities are appropriate at any point of the lesson—beginning, middle, or end. But beware; especially if you are the artsy-craftsy type. You will be tempted to try this great art project you recently read about. After all, the kids will love it. But, if an art activity does not materially contribute to the achievement of your learning objectives, then it is not a Bible Learning Activity and should not be used, no matter how great it is.

Here are a few suggestions for art activities:

• PAINTING with a variety of paints on any of a hundred different surfaces (especially the tables and floors) with brushes, sponges, fingers, toes, string, etc.

• PRINTING with rollers and linoleum blocks, carved potatoes, hand or thumb prints, or calligraphy.

• DRAWING with crayons, chalk, charcoals, pencils, etc.

• Making COLLAGES and BANNERS with a variety of materials.

• SCULPTURING with clay, styrofoam, chenille wire, etc.

4. MUSIC: Of all the Bible Learning Activities used with children, none intimidates teachers as much as music. But no other one has the same powerful impact on children as music. Unfortunately, adults often perceive themselves as having no musical ability, thus they shy away from using music more than absolutely necessary.

But that is the adult's problem. Children of elementary school age have few musical prejudices. Watch them. As they work alone on a project, it is only a very short time before they begin singing or humming or chanting. Often, when several are working together they spontaneously will begin singing, accompanied by smiles and giggles. This is especially true of the girls, or among children who attend music classes together in school.

This lack of inhibitions in music is a beautifully natural form of expression that God has given. The great accompanying benefit is that they accept you as one of them, musically speaking. You don't have to be an accomplished singer to lead meaningful music BLAs. All you have to have is a willing spirit.

So think of music as a Bible Learning Activity, not as a component to a song service. Make music a learning tool. Here are a few suggestions:

• Songs help children learn Scripture, either the Biblical concepts or word-for-word. For instance, "Be Strong and of Good Courage" is Joshua 1:9 verbatim.

• Songs help children worship by setting a mood of quiet and reverence. Songs often focus on a particular attribute of God or a particular response (usually praise) that we can make to God.

• Songs reinforce a childs view of Christian living. A singable melody and easy-to-remember words often pop up when least expected but most needed! By allowing children to write new verses to familiar melodies, further reinforcement is gained. They will write about their own experiences, from their own backgrounds. Expressing the truth of Scripture in a song verse means expressing how they see the truth affecting their lives.

• Music provides a wonderful audio backdrop to other activities. Music playing quietly in the background soothes the clamour that arises when all the children in your department are busy working. Playing a song also can be a signal that one part of the class session is ending and another is about to begin. If used every week in the same way the ringing of bells is used in schools to signal class changes, children pick up the routine and transitions are made much more smoothly.

5. DRAMA: Have you ever dressed up like a clown, full face makeup and all? Or have you ever, as an adult, put on a full-face mask for any length of time? There is something about dressing up or dressing differently that allows us to express ourselves in ways we never would in our normal clothes and environment. Drama as a Bible Learning Activity takes advantage of this human propensity for climbing into someone else's shoes and living for a short time in an imaginary world.

Acting out a Bible story requires that children first know the Bible story. Then, acting it out allows them to experience the story in a way that rarely happens when the story is merely told. And, acting out the story provides you with a great teaching opportunity as you explore the events, characters, feelings, motives, and outcome.

As you guide drama activities, keep the cardinal rule of BLAs ever before you: the important element is not a high quality show you will stage for parents or even other children. The important element is the process of digging into the story, talking about it, and synthesizing what is learned into dramatic play.

In addition to these few ideas, your curriculum will have many others with guidelines for lesson-related use:

- ACT out Bible stories
- PANTOMIME
- ROLEPLAY
- PUPPETS

A SUGGESTION: Even though you won't use drama every week, it is helpful to have a box of costume material in your room. Large pieces of curtain or drapes; different shapes and colors of material; belts, headbands, and other tie-items; sandals or thongs; unusual hats or wraps for headdressings; a variety of items that could be used as props.

6. MISCELLANEOUS Bible Learning Activities include puzzles, Bible games, displays, field trips, service projects, and anything else your imagination comes up with or your curriculum suggests. But remember: They must be lesson-related to qualify. The few minutes we have with children each week require that faithful stewardship.

Bible Learning Activities for the Youth Department

1. VERBAL ACTIVITIES: People love to talk! Especially teens, who even though they have spent the day together still can find an inexhaustible well of words to fill hours on a telephone each evening.

Expressing oneself is as important to the learning process as the bringing in of new ideas. In fact, it is the other side of the same coin. New ideas and information become my ideas and information only when they are processed and accepted. In order to express himself in a way that is satisfying, a teen must first have good information and then process it internally so that s/he owns it and can express it. Thus, expression and ownership go hand in hand.

The variety of verbal activities is very wide. Consider a few:

- DISCUSSION: True discussion occurs when learners discuss ideas with one another, guided by the teacher but interacting mainly with one another. Youth discussion is a blend of true discussion along with "question and answer." Groups of six to eight teens respond to your carefully worded questions, and occasionally talk to one another about the topic under consideration. But their comments generally are directed to you or through you to the group. That makes the quality of your questions a very important element of any discussion. They have to be clear, nonthreatening , and understandable. Also, you should gear your questions to stimulate teens to think about what God was doing with the people in a Bible story and what God is doing in their hearts.
- BRAINSTORMING: This is simply asking, "Let's list as many different ______ as we can in two minutes." They love it and you'll be surprised at their resourcefulness!
- AGREE/DISAGREE: A statement is made and the learners have to state whether they agree with the statement or

disagree with it, then explain why. Let individuals respond, or let pairs or trios respond.

• CIRCLE RESPONSE: A clearly worded question is asked, one which is open-ended, such as, "What type of peer presure is the most difficult to resist?" Time is given to formulate an answer, then answers are given, in turn, around the circle.

• STORYTELLING: Are you surprised? Most teachers of this age seldom think of storytelling as a teaching tool. But don't you love a good story? Don't your teens? Try telling the Bible story with drama and enthusiasm. Use a story about modern teens to set up a problem which your learners solve by applying the Biblical truth of the day's lesson. Storytelling isn't just for children. Don't forget that teens love to tell stories, too. When you combine the storytelling with art activities in which they create visuals to go along with their stories, you have a great formula for learning.

2. WRITING ACTIVITIES: Yes, this includes filling in the spaces in the handouts you distribute in class. But stretch your horizons! Writing is a great way to help teens think about the Bible truth you are studying. The old adage among writers is, "You can't write it if you don't understand it." Writing your thoughts requires more mental effort than simply speaking them because it requires more understanding of the subject of your thoughts.

Writing activities are great, but remember that it's the making of the cake that is important, not the cake itself. You are not a school teacher charged with correcting errors to produce laureates. You are charged with reaching and teaching people to know God.

Consider using a few of these different writing activities:

• JOURNAL: Your learners will enjoy writing a journal during a study of a character's life that stretches over several weeks, or that lasts only one week. Teens are used to learning vicariously. They love adventure stories and tales from history. Their imaginations are still vivid enough to put themselves in others' places. Ask teens to write a "Dear Diary" entry from the main character's point of view. Or assign each teen a different character from the story. Or create a situation in life today in which a person experiences something similar to that which the Bible character experienced, then let the group write from that person's perspective.

• NEWSPAPER: Work together to publish a JERUSALEM TIMES or a BETHLEHEM HERALD or the like. Different teens write the various sections of the paper. They'll not only want to write it, They'll want to lay it out, provide graphics, and print it. If that meets your learning objective.

• POETRY: There is traditional verse. They write it all or you provide one verse, they provide the next, as individuals or as a group. There is also free verse and haiku which is three lines with a specific number of syllables in each line (five, seven, and five, unrhymed).

Also consider:

• REWRITING PARABLES;
• WRITING LETTERS to or from Bible characters;
• BOOK REPORTS;
• RESEARCH AND REPORT;
• GRAFFITTI;
• LISTS.

A HINT: In using writing activities, you should be aware of the wide differences in the ability and interest levels of your teens. It's OK if John chooses not to write. There's a reason. Involve him in helping roles to minimize his self-consciousness, as well as the havoc he could create in your group.

3. ART: This is a perennial favorite of childrens' teachers, but a category of activities often overlooked by youth teachers. Because this category is limited only by your own imagination, we'll simply lay out a few concepts and list a variety of art media. You can do the rest (your curriculum will give you lots of help, too).

Here are a few suggestions for art activities:

- PAINTING with a variety of paints on any of a hundred different surfaces (especially the tables and floors) with brushes, sponges, string, etc.
- PRINTING with rollers and linoleum blocks, carved potatoes, hand or thumb prints, or calligraphy.
- DRAWING with crayons, chalk, charcoals, pencils, etc.
- Making COLLAGES, MURALS, and BANNERS with different kinds of materials.
- SCULPTURING with clay, styrofoam, chenille wire, etc.
- Using PHOTOGRAPHY, SLIDE MAKING, VIDEO PRODUCTION, or FILMSTRIP CREATION as learning activities for teens.
- DESIGNING bumper stickers or cartoons which inject humor in the lesson.

4. MUSIC: Music is one of the most powerful influences in teens' lives because it is ever present in their environment. Using music as a learning activity is an enjoyable experience for teens, provided the activity is simple, clearly explained, and provides little opportunity for embarrassment before peers.

Youth leaders often shy away from using music because they are themselves self-conscious. They perceive themselves as having no musical abilities. However, teens live with music constantly. Why not use this universal language to help them think about God's Word?

Think of music as a Bible Learning Activity, helpful in learning Scripture, worshipping, and thinking about their lives and culture. Here are a few ideas:

- WRITE a verse to a familiar tune.
- SING a song to learn a Bible passage.
- LISTEN to Christian music to discuss.
- MAKE UP COMMERCLALS for Bible concepts using familiar themes of popular products.

5. DRAMA: Have you ever dressed up like a clown, full face makeup and all? Or have you ever, as an adult, put on a full-face mask for any length of time? There is something about dressing up or dressing differently that allows us to express ourselves in ways we never would in our normal clothes and environment. Drama as a Bible Learning Activity takes advantage of this human propensity for climbing into another's shoes, even if just for fun.

Teens love drama if you introduce it in a way that minimizes their self-consciousness. They typically act out their thoughts and feelings more than adults because they do not have the range of vocabulary with which to express themselves.

Think of using the following activities to meaningfully reinforce your lesson theme:

- PLAYS to depict the Bible lesson or a modern parallel.
- PANTOMIMES or ROLEPLAYS respond to a problem the lesson addresses.
- SKITS portray action.
- TV SHOWS provide creativity.

6. MISCELLANEOUS: Finally the

catch-all for those round pegs among all these square holes is miscellaneous. Try crossword-type puzzles, creating or presenting displays or exhibits, giving tests or quizzes, building models, etc. The possibilities are endless!

Bible Learning Activities for the Adult Division

1. VERBAL ACTIVITIES: People love to talk! It's a basic human gift and a deep human need. And in the learning process, expressing oneself is as important as the bringing in of new ideas. In fact, it is the other side of the same coin. New ideas and information become my ideas and information only when they are processed and accepted. In order to express himself in a way that is satisfying, an adult must first have good input and then process it internally so that s/he owns it and can express it. Thus, expression and ownership go hand in hand.

The variety of Verbal Activities is very wide. Consider a few:

• DISCUSSION: True discussion occurs when learners discuss ideas with one another, guided by the teacher but interacting mainly with one another. Adult discussion sometimes is like that, while it sometimes is question and answer. Other times it is a blend of true discussion and question and answer. Use the variety to best advantage, but remember: in all discussion, the quality of your questions is a key element for success. Your questions must be clear, non-threatening , and understandable. You should gear them to stimulate your learners to consider what God was doing in the lives of the people in the Bible passage you are studying, as well as what God is doing in the world today.

• BRAINSTORMING: This is simply saying, "Let's list as many different ______ as we can in two minutes." They love it! You'll be surprised at their resourcefulness!

• AGREE/DISAGREE: A statement is made and learners have to state whether they agree with the statement or disagree with it, then explain why. Let individuals respond, or let pairs or trios respond.

• CIRCLE RESPONSE: A clearly worded question is asked, which is open-ended such as, "What type of social pressure is the most difficult for you to resist?" Time is given to formulate an answer, then answers are given, in turn, around the circle.

• LECTURE: Lecture is a wonderful teaching tool when it is used to accomplish the tasks it does best. Use it to communicate a large amount of information in a short amount of time. Use it to summarize one part of a class discussion or project. Or use it to make a transition from one activity to another. Lecture is also useful for inspiation—nothing lifts and challenges like a good speech.

• STORYTELLING: Are you surprised? Most adult teachers seldom think of storytelling as a teaching tool. But don't you love a good story? Try telling the Bible story with drama and enthusiasm. Use a story about a modern version of the same situation to set up a problem which your learners solve by applying the Biblical truth of the day's lesson. Storytelling isn't just for children. But don't imagine that you are the only one who should tell the stories. Get others involved.

2. WRITING ACTIVITIES: Yes, this includes taking notes on the profound depths of insight you pour forth in your weekly lectures. But stretch your horizons! Writing is a great way to help adults think

about the Bible truth you are studying. The old adage among writers is, "You can't write it if you don't understand it." Writing your thoughts requires more mental effort than simply speaking them because it requires more understanding of the subject of your thoughts.

Writing activities are great, but remember that It's the making of the cake that is important, not the cake itself. You are not a literary critic judging the quality of the learner.s work. You are charged with reaching and teaching people to know God.

Consider using a few of these writing activities:

• JOURNAL: Your learners will enjoy writing a journal during a study of a character's life that stretches over several weeks, or that lasts only one week. Adults are used to learning vicariously. They easily put themselves into others' places. Ask learners to write a "Dear Diary" entry from the main character's point of view. Or assign each small group a different character from the story. Or create a situation in life today in which a person experiences something similar to that which the Bible character experienced, then let the group write from that person's perspective.

• NEWSPAPER ARTICLES: To recreate the setting of a story so a clearer understanding of its meaning can emerge, allow learners to become reporters and ask the basic questions: Who , What, When, Where, Why, and How. Then let them write up the account as if they were correspondents with United Press International. Of course, they then read their work to the group.

• POETRY: There is traditional verse—they write it all or you provide one verse and they provide the next. There is also free verse and haiku (three lines with a specific number of syllables in each line: five, seven, and five, unrhymed).

Also consider:

• REWRITING PARABLES
• WRITING LETTERS to or from the Biblical character
• BOOK REPORTS
• RESEARCH AND REPORT
• LISTS

3. ART: A perennial favorite of children's teachers, but a category of activities often overlooked by teachers of adults—this category is limited only by your own imagination. We'll simply lay out a few concepts and list a variety of art media. You do the rest (your curriculum will give you lots of help, too).

Art activities are appropriate at any point of the lesson—beginning, middle, or end. Once you discover how much adults enjoy them, you will be tempted to try this new approach. However, if an art activity does not materially contribute to the achievement of your learning objectives, then it is not a Bible Learning Activity and should not be used no matter how great it is.

Here are a few suggestions for art activities:

• PAINTING OR DRAWING coats of arms for Bible characters or class members;

• Making COLLAGES, MURALS, and BANNERS with different kinds of materials.

• Using PHOTOGRAPHY, SLIDE MAKING, VIDEO PRODUCTION, or FILMSTRIP CREATION as Bible learning activities.

• DESIGNING bumper stickers or cartoons which inject humor in the lesson.

4. MUSIC–Music has power! Consider these important contributions music could make to your class:

- Songs help people learn Scripture
- Songs help people worship.
- Songs reinforce the learners' view of Christian living.

• Music provides a wonderful backdrop for other activities. Quiet music playing behind group projects or discussions is often appreciated.

Adult teachers often shy away from using music because they are self-conscious. They perceive themselves as having no musical abilities. That's OK! If you are too shy to lead music, recruit one of the many accomplished musicians in your class to help. Why not use this universal language to help adults think about God's Word?

Think of music as a Bible Learning Activity. It is helpful for teaching Scripture, worshipping, and thinking about their lives. Here are a few ideas:

- WRITE a new verse to a familiar tune
- SING a song together to learn a Bible passage
- LISTEN to Christian music to analyze and discuss.

• CREATE commercials for Bible concepts using familiar themes of popular products.

5. DRAMA: Have you ever dressed up like a clown, full face makeup and all? Or have you ever, as an adult, put on a full-face mask for any length of time? There is something about dressing up or dressing differently that allows us to express ourselves in ways we never would in our normal clothes and environment. Drama as a Bible Learning Activity takes advantage of this human propensity for climbing into another's shoes, even if just for fun.

Adults enjoy drama if you introduce it in a way that minimizes their self-consciousness. The age-old popularity of charades and the recent revival of that form of drama with drawings instead of pantomime proves that acting is fun. Think of using the following activities to meaningfully reinforce your lesson theme:

- PLAYS, depict the Bible story or a modern parallel.
- PANTOMIMES or ROLEPLAYS respond to a problem.
- SKITS portray action.
- TV SHOWS provide creativity.

6. MISCELLANEOUS: Finally the catch all for those round pegs among all these square holes is miscellaneous. Think of using crossword-type puzzles, creating or presenting displays or exhibits, giving tests or quizzes, building models, etc.